LIFTING THE LID

Interviews with concert pianists

MICHAEL JOHNSON
and
FRANCES WILSON

Published by

Lagrange Group

Bordeaux, France

email: johnson33@laposte.net

ISBN : 978-2-9590554-2-3

Book designed and produced by Laurence Mignard.

Acknowledgements

We were privileged to speak with the great talents featured in this book, and are grateful for the thought and time they invested in their contributions. We thank them for their cooperation, their candour, their expertise, and sometimes their humour.

Contents

Introduction

Classical pianists have an unmistakable mystique about them. More often than not, alone on the stage with just that box of wood and wires for company, stretched before the performer like a sleek black limousine, pianists seem more removed, almost other-worldly, than other classical musicians.

There is a great curiosity about what classical musicians do, not just their life on the concert platform - the visible, public aspect of the profession - but 'what musicians do all day', as it were. A certain urban mythology surrounds the working life of the concert pianist; we may imagine them slaving away at their instrument for hours on end, cut off from family, a social life, or the normal activities of daily life. For how else could these people learn and finesse so many notes, so many details, in order to bring the music alive for us in performance and on countless recordings?

In reality, the life of the concert pianist today is rather different from the clichéd image of the wild-haired virtuoso, confined to their practice room or studio with only the instrument and its literature for company. A startling level of commitment and executive function is required to learn, memorise and perform complex music. Added to that, the profession today is highly competitive, tough, often lonely. Yet as these interviews reveal, the instrument and its repertoire exert a strong attraction, seducing would-be professionals from a young age and continuing to bewitch, delight, frustrate and excite. Some give their advice on how to function in the piano world. Christine Croshaw put it best: "Be curious. Allow yourself to experiment. Be kind to yourself. Embrace uncertainty... Follow your dreams... Enjoy the journey."

The interviews in this book offer remarkable and often surprisingly honest insights into life as a professional pianist today, giving readers a glimpse beyond the notes and the concert stage to the daily exigencies of being a pianist – from years of intense study with some of the leading pianist-teachers and pedagogues of our time to practicing and performing, repertoire and recording. There are also more esoteric reflections on the nature of "success" as a musician, and advice for young musicians who are considering a professional career. Boris Giltburg feels he is successful if he helps the audience "forget their troubles and be transported to wherever the music can take them."

Ivo Pogorelich, who has attracted the extremes of praise and criticism during his long career, calls life “a struggle”. So how does he define perfect happiness? “Not seeking it on purpose.”

Some of the world’s greatest living concert pianists are included here - amongst them, Marc-André Hamelin, Stephen Hough, Joanna MacGregor, François-Frédéric Guy, Tamara Stefanovich and Pogorelich himself. We have also included interviews with lesser-known pianists and younger artists who are beginning to make their mark on the international stage, including Vikingur Olafsson and Pavel Kolesnikov.

The interviews have been selected from face-to-face meetings conducted by Michael Johnson before and after concerts and at music festivals, and from Frances Wilson’s popular Meet the Artist series, launched on her blog The Cross-Eyed Pianist in 2012 and now comprising a significant archive of over 500 interviews with players, composers and conductors active today.

Following in the footsteps of titles such as Dean Elder’s Pianists at Play and David Dubal’s Reflections from the Keyboard, Lifting the Lid is an important survey of the thoughts and attitudes of today’s professional pianists and a significant resource for all those who are fascinated by the piano and those who play it.

Michael Johnson & Frances Wilson

Bordeaux and London

Portraits by Michael Johnson

Interviews by Michael Johnson

Marc-André Hamelin

I must bore some people - I don't move when I play

The late Heinrich Neuhaus wrote in 'The Art of Piano Playing' that "confidence is the prerequisite of freedom" in piano playing and that "pianophobia" affects inexperienced players who lack confident technique. Does this sound familiar?

Yes, playing is a little like expressing yourself in a new language. When you don't know the language completely you stumble and don't have the freedom to express yourself as you might wish without having to think of the nitty-gritty of the grammar. Music works the same way.

Where do you go looking for these underrated composers?

I just have to go into the next room.

You have your own private collection?

Last time we moved I had 87 boxes, all catalogued.

You have had success in your composition efforts, specifically your 12 etudes. Are you still able to find the time to compose?

Well, my etudes took so long because there was a gap of 12 years in the middle. I was constantly being asked by friends when I would finish them. Actually I have tons of unfinished things - some which should never see the light I day. But finally I wrote the last three a few years ago and now they are published.

Did you stop performing while finishing off the etudes?

Oh no. I usually write away from the piano. I can work on a plane, in a hotel room.

Do parts of your compositions come to you in dreams, as Stravinsky claimed of himself?

That happened once. And then a couple of years ago I tried improvising. Then I wrote down the piece as it came out.

Isn't that a terribly painstaking exercise?

Oh no, I love it. I used software to bring the tempo down to an absolute crawl.

Does contemporary music attract you? Your recordings seem to lean toward the traditional.

Thanks to my father, who had a good selection of scores, I was familiar with traditional repertoire at an early age, so my next step (as a young pianist) was composers such as Stockhausen, Boulez, Schoenberg and John Cage.

I'm still involved with that period. I played in the Cage Centennial. I even did the famous *4'33"*. At one point I was walking across the stage whistling Satie. Among others involved were Meredith Monk, Joan La Barbara and Jessye Norman. It was a lot of fun.

Yet your discography does not include music from living composers.

No, going back to contemporary music would be almost like a full-time dedication for me. I don't just want to do it selectively. Something like Feldman was different. When I sat down to read *For Bunita Marcus* I was thunderstruck. It's a self-contained universe. As you're playing, it becomes obvious nothing else beyond it even exists. To be able to create this is quite miraculous.

Are audiences coming around?

People respond to it differently. I warned one friend he might not like Feldman. After a few minutes of my playing it, he got out his cellphone and started reading *The Economist.*

You complained in a 'Clavier Companion' interview that young players are guilty of histrionics at the keyboard. If this is a trend, how can a controlled player like you compete?

I often wonder... I must bore some people because I don't move when I play. Some people take this as emotional detachment but my contention is that one should come to concerts to listen, not to watch. I can assure you that you will not learn anything by watching me. Reproducing my gestures just wouldn't work. When I watch myself on video, there's a disconnect between what I see and what I felt at the time. It always looks effortless, like I'm just brushing the keys, but there is force at work, a lot of force.

You are an advocate of broad outside interests in young players. If you think of other things, what might they be?

I don't consider myself a man of great culture, but if I had somehow never discovered my aptitude for the piano, I might have done something in language, like translation, writing. The time we have on this Earth is scandalously short. I make the most of it within my limits.

If your time ran out unexpectedly, what would you want to be remembered for?

I want to be remembered for bringing music to the public and for making a little bit of a dent as far as repertoire discovery is concerned.

Marc-André HAMELIN

Rudolf Buchbinder

30 years ago I was not free like this

Austrian pianist Rudolf (Rudi) Buchbinder performed the five Beethoven piano concertos while conducting the Sachsische Staatskapelle of Dresden from the keyboard. He accomplished in a single day, showing no sign of strain, remarkable feat for a player of 72 years of age. In our interview, he was relaxed and cheerful and spoke freely. He dismissed his marathon feat of keyboard conducting as "nothing special". An edited transcript of our conversation follows.

You have performed the five Beethoven piano concertos, conducting from the keyboard, several times. Doesn't this make you a specialist in music marathons?

Actually, a solo recital is much worse than plain the five. Even practicing for four hours is much worse. I once played the two Brahms concertos in one evening !

But you also conduct from the keyboard. That must be stressful.

This is nothing special. Before, everybody did it. Beethoven did it. I conduct with my eyes, with my mouth, a little bit with my hands. I have done it 500 times in my life. It's a different kind of concentration. The players have to listen.

You are not intimidated by such a large task?

No. Why should I be?

Well, there are a lot of notes!

Oh no. The secret of piano playing is simple. You just have to touch the right notes at the right time. That's it [*Laughs*].

Do you have a favourite among the five?

No. If I had a favourite, I could not play the others. It's my problem. I have to love all of them. Each concerto is completely different.

Aren't they derived from Mozart's piano concertos in certain passages? Tovey wrote of "several examples of Mozart" that appear in No. 1. These two geniuses were rivals.

People say the first two concertos are influenced by Mozart but that's not true. They have nothing to do with Mozart. It's all about Beethoven. Beethoven didn't think about Mozart. In fact, he hated Mozart. When he came to Vienna, Mozart was God. It took Beethoven a long time to be as popular. People also try to make three periods in the Beethoven sonatas. Wrong. He had his ups and downs throughout this life.

RUDOLF BUCHBINDER

You compose cadenzas for other concertos but you do not use your own for the Beethoven concertos?

No… only Beethoven's. They are not so bad, you know [*Laughs*].

A personal question about your stamina. At age 72, can you play all five without worrying about fatigue?

I admit that am very nervous. The older I get, the more nervous I get. As a young man, I used to walk on stage confidently. [*Stands up and mime confident postures, as if marching on stage.*]

You don't worry about this increasing nervousness?

No. No. Backstage, I don't think about the concert that is coming. When I come onstage, I have cold fingers. A few seconds later, at the keyboard, I am back to normal.

Do you worry about memory lapses ?

No. This should never happen. I am very secure. Well, maybe a little bit in Mozart's K466.

Do you have ten years left, or twenty, like Badura-Skoda, who played into his 90s?

Look. I have to play. But I only play when I am able to concentrate. I only practice two hours a day, but sometimes I don't touch the piano for one week.

Is playing getting more difficult or easier?

The Brahms concertos are much easier for me now than ten years ago. I played the Tchaikovsky First with Valery Gergiev maybe five or six times and also Rachmaninoff.

Critics and other experts like to identify Beethoven's development from Classical composing to a more Romantic style. Where does this begin to happen?

This is stupid. The first one is Romantic. Beethoven always went up and down throughout his life. Beethoven was the most romantic composer in music history. He is the only composer who writes *espressivo a tempo*. Nobody else. He leaves the freedom to the interpreter.

Is this a freedom that you can express now because of your age and experience? Does this empower you to say what you really think, regardless of other opinions?

You know the late Joachim Kaiser? We knew each other very, very well.

He forced me... he said to me, "Rudi, you have to record the Beethoven sonatas again." After 30 years interval I did them again for Sony in Dresden and then again at the Salzburg Festival. Thirty years ago I was not "free" like this.

And when did you feel this freedom?

You cannot control it. It comes by itself. Like in the Hammerklavier, you play fast [*Sings the opening phrase, loudly and vigorously*] like B-DUM PATA DUM PATA DUMDUM. You play those first seven or eight bars by the metronome, and then you are free. Beethoven writes everything very clearly. After that introduction he keeps the pedal. That makes a big difference. Many players do not have those freedoms today. They are afraid. Beethoven writes *rinf forzando* (slurring), for the whole phrase. Only Brahms also used *rinf.* The alternative is *fortepiano*, which is short, like a mosquito bite.

But you have discovered the freedom. Aren't you afraid of criticism?

I have no problem with criticism. If the critic declares what is right and what is wrong. What I don't like is the critic who says, for no reason, "It was too fast."

You always choose Steinways for your concerts. Why not Bösendorfer, for example, or Fazioli?

Of course Vienna was very proud of Bösendorfer. But the tone to me is much too sharp, too harsh. Bösendorfer makes its own sound. I want to make the sound myself.

"Too glassy", as some pianists say.

Steinway is the most neutral of all pianos. By this I mean that nothing comes from the piano, the way it is built. How you treat a woman like the Steinway, it's the same. When you treat them good, they respond good. What you give, it comes back. I want to make the sound. You can play soft, you can play lyrically, *espressivo*. The range is much bigger.

You have said you want to die on the keyboard?

Yes, like Wilhelm Backhaus. After two movements of a Schubert *Impromptu* he left the stage, then returned to play the same thing over again. It was his favourite. He was very ill and knew This would be his final performance. After his Schubert, he was taken to hospital where he died.

Kyle Gann

No one knows what's good in new music

You once encouraged open-mindedness toward new sound-worlds. Do you see other musicians or music-lovers agreeing, and demonstrating real tolerance for newness?

Oh, open-mindedness as a virtue in itself is very popular at the moment, insofar as it means not discriminating against other musical genres. A tolerance for real newness is much rarer. The great tragedy is that, collectively, musicians long ago decided that no one knows what's good in new music anyway.

We used to know good from bad.

The main cause, I think, was the scholarly embrace of Schoenberg and his disciples, which disastrously shook people's confidence in their own ears. The unfortunate upshot is that, if you do something new that's so abstract or complicated that no one understands it, the musical elites tend to give it the benefit of the doubt. If you do something new and they can understand it, they dismiss it as "Well, it's not going to catch on."

What do you mean by catching on?

"Catching on" means success, and our musical elites critique musical trends the way op-ed writers review political races, not to judge anything on merit but to keep score of who's winning. So there is a glib tolerance for a certain type of vague newness, but not toward anything clear-cut.

Examples?

Take microtonality, minimalism, and pop influences. Microtonality "just doesn't sound good" to people who haven't taken the time to get used to it or seek out the best of it. Minimalism remains widely frowned upon in music composition programmes, disdained on principle for its very popular success. Pop influences in new music are frowned upon even by younger composers who love pop music, which blows my mind.

Going back to Cowell and Cage, the rejection of the European music traditions has been a constant in the new music world. Surely you don't hate Beethoven, Schubert, Brahms, Liszt ... do you?

Almost every composer loves all that music, but it is tragic to live (as those composers didn't) in a concert-going world in which 95 per cent of the music made public is from the distant past.

KYLE
GANN

I've stolen as many devices from Beethoven, Bruckner, Schubert, and Liszt as any composer living, but I have no patience for concerts at which only that music is played. Mozart is wonderful, but I would far rather live in a new creative world analogous to his than live as a tourist endlessly visiting a preserved simulacrum of his world every day.

Isn't "beautiful music" a personal matter, a subjective term?

The subjectivity of beauty in music has been greatly overstated. Any music or art or literature, when it first appears, may find public resonance for a variety of subjective reasons. Eventually, though, the social reasons for that resonance will fade away, and under close collective scrutiny the quality of a piece will gradually become evident.

Speaking as a composer, you do not believe music comes out of thin air, do you?

I'm always acutely aware how much inspiration comes from the materials any composer is working with. You push notes, and they push back - you place a sound in your imagination, and when played it sounds like something you didn't expect. Ives, for example, was in the first generation to encounter Helmholtz's 'On the Sensations of Tone', and (like Debussy and others) he was becoming aware of the overtone series, both as spiritual metaphor and as a template for new approaches to harmony and rhythm.

Wouldn't young composers of today benefit from aligning themselves with a philosophical ethos in order to find their musical way?

It's an interesting question, but open to interpretation. My impulse is to answer yes. When young I did a tremendous amount of reading in the history of aesthetics, and as a result my sense of artist - ethos, necessity, whatever - is not limited to post-WWII influences. One result is that I've never had any patience for the late-20th-century idea that art is about "personal expression."

Does corporate control of the music business squeeze out creative work? Won't creative urges always find a way to break free?

The first question rather answers itself, doesn't it? Since at least Kant, art has been defined as disinterested pleasure, and if you're doing it with an eye to make money, that's no longer disinterested. And the second question is economic. Artists need resources, collaborative aid, and opportunities to do their work and make it public. Creative urges always break free, but if they are denied realisation and access to a public forum, they are sometimes squelched at birth.

Do your composer friends continue producing (in the Charles Ives tradition) in the belief that an audience is out there, we just have to find it or wait for it to catch up?

Of course there's an audience out there, for almost anything - if corporations put enough money behind it to expose it widely. In 1992 Nonesuch records made Gorecki's then-seventeen-year-old 'Symphony of Sorrowful Songs' famous by sending it out to a wide range of tastemakers and celebrities. I think it's a mediocre piece, and that its appeal will dwindle.

What is your relationship with the piano? You dropped it and stopped practicing some years ago. That must have left a huge void. Will you return to it one day?

No. I don't have the discipline to sit there and work at it long enough to get good enough to enjoy it again. I do miss it, but I started typing instead, which became a more manageable substitute.

You have written a lot of piano music, including transcriptions. Is this the focus of your activity now?

Writing words was what replaced performance. I'm not a performer-type personality; my brain slips up, forgets, and stutters. I do that in writing too, but no one can tell from the edited end result. I do write a lot of keyboard transcriptions, in order to thoroughly understand some pieces I love.

Where do you see the future of your music going? Do you see it gaining more and more recognition?

In the last few years my music has completely fallen off the map. Except for a small frisson that "Hyperchromatica" seems to have created among young microtonalists, interest in my music has settled around zero. There are many plausible reasons: I'm a white male in an identity-politics era, my approach to microtonality is too baffling, everyone ignores composers who haven't become brand names by a certain age, I live in the boondocks, I'm not a "people person." At the moment I can't stand the thought of putting energy into something no one will perform. Perhaps this will change again.

Do you wonder how you will be remembered when your time comes? Do you care?

Emphatically yes to all three. Matthew Arnold argued, in 'Culture and Anarchy' I think, that great art requires not only the artist capable of it but the right cultural moment in which to realise and receive it. I've learned by my age that an artist's most copious and exemplary accomplishments can effectively add up to nothing if the society of the time is not receptive to them.

I could name quite a number of composers from the past whose music I think has been unjustifiably excluded from "the canon." I can't doubt that I have achieved something worthwhile, and I'm tired of speculating why my ideas have achieved such spotty resonance.

Yet you are a household name among switched-on musicians!

I could do worse than to end up like Erik Satie, with a wide following but eternally considered a fringe figure. During my lifetime I have had a certain underground reputation, though the professional music world has become closed off to me, one might say adamantly and on ideological grounds. Those are the possibilities. But past a certain age, recognition can aid only one's vanity.

Ivan Ilic

Ultimately, I'm a loner

How old were you when you discovered you could make music on the piano?

I started lessons at age six. We had a Baldwin upright piano at home and hearing my sister practice fascinated me. I played with the piano early on, and when I turned six, I began lessons with the same teacher. Soon afterwards he told my parents that I had an unusual talent.

What was your father's profession?

My father earned a doctorate in physics at Stanford University following a master's in electrical engineering in Belgrade, where he was the youngest student to ever enroll. He was then briefly an assistant professor at Stanford before taking a job in Silicon Valley.

You are one of those musicians who studied mathematics and music at the same time. Were you strong in maths from an early age?

Yes. I grew up near Stanford, and the public school system was unusually competitive: they tested students for aptitude, constantly. I always tested in the top percentile in maths. I also enjoyed it from the beginning; it was always like a game to me. Advanced mathematics is a different story. You have to enjoy struggling with elusive concepts, and most people get discouraged. To my surprise, I enjoyed it the more difficult it got.

Did the University of California at Berkeley encourage you to stay with maths, to teach maths, to work in applied science rather than music?

My professors knew I wasn't going to pursue maths because I skipped lectures and just took the exams, studying on my own. I'll never forget my maths graduation ceremony, when my Russian professor of Complex Analysis found out that the reason I skipped his lectures was that I was an aspiring musician, not because I was lazy. When he found out I was leaving for Paris to pursue music, it was the only time I saw him smile.

Was there a sudden revelation that determined music as your calling?

No, nothing sudden. At university, I began attending music classes assiduously and spending my time in practice rooms. I wanted to absorb all things musical. I couldn't even say it was a choice because it didn't feel like one.

What kept you in the more precarious world of music?

In the music lectures, I was excited by everything. For example, my first university-level music course was about Middle Eastern music. I learned to sing in Arabic, recognize Umm Kulthum's voice immediately, and play basic Middle Eastern percussion rhythms. I was even infatuated with a classmate, an Egyptian named Dina. Equally, I took a class on Brahms given by a distinguished professor emeritus who took delight in introducing masterpieces like the Horn Trio to oblivious students. Or musicianship classes which involved singing the oboe parts of Bach cantatas while other students read the figured bass. Or combative musicological readings of history by Richard Taruskin, one of the most inspiring musical minds I have encountered.

What were you playing at this stage ?

I was deep into Bach partitas, Chopin etudes and Beethoven sonatas, and was asked to premiere student and faculty pieces, and play in the orchestra. It was inspiring and a broader education than I had imagined possible.

How did you end up at the Paris Conservatory? Was there a teacher that you wanted to study with?

The year before I finished college, I spent eight weeks at a summer festival in Aspen, and my roommate was French. We became friends and he helped spark my interest in France. The plan was to stay for a year, then attend graduate school in the US. I applied to the Conservatory and, to my surprise, I was accepted. My first year in Paris, paid for by a scholarship, eliminated any desire to return to the United States.

You studied with the eccentric René Duchâble.

I saw a flyer in Paris for masterclasses with him, so I applied and was accepted. I then travelled to Annecy, his home, to visit and work with him a few times a year. Then I became a part of his small class at the École Normale, for one year. He was generous with me, and expansive in his lessons, but also practical. He doesn't have a premeditated pedagogy, which meant that he was like an older brother showing me how to do tricks on a motorcycle. I loved that fraternal aspect of working with him.

Why did you part company?

I increasingly felt the need to find my own way, and I subsequently lost touch with him and all my teachers over the years. Ultimately I'm a loner and feel one is better off learning the most important musical lessons alone. The only teacher I am still regularly in touch with is the one with whom I studied for my first 10 years, who still lives in Palo Alto, and whom I adore - probably because he let me follow my instincts and didn't try to mold me into something I didn't want to become.

IVAN ILIĆ

Your first recitals and CDs focused on Debussy, Haydn, Liszt. But weren't you also interested in contemporary music?

My interest in contemporary music started at university, and I took to it immediately. I gave premieres of new chamber and solo works. Frankly, it felt easy to me, compared to traditional repertoire. Other musicians seemed intimidated by the complexity, but compared to my maths classes the musical complexity was a joke.

Are you collaborating with living composers?

Yes, Scott Wollschleger sends me unfinished new works every month. Keeril Makan is working on a piano concerto. Melaine Dalibert has dedicated several recent works to me. There are more names on the horizon. But these are the three where I feel I can have a big impact on their careers, and all three write music that I feel born to play.

Who starts the process and how closely do you work together?

Usually they send me fragments or finished works, as Wollschleger does. I record myself practicing them with my phone, and share via instant messages, very early on, to check if I'm on the right track. Sometimes they provide hints, sometimes detailed discussions ensue, and sometimes I suggest changes.

You have become known as a pianist who brings neglected works to the fore. Is this your main thrust now? Do you have other revelations in the wings?

I have a list, a pipeline in progress, of works that I plan to record or perform which I think of as 'just below the surface' in terms of notoriety. Scientists have made the point that although colonizing outer space captures the public's imagination, the ocean contains such a multitude of species and landscapes that are mostly hidden in deep, inaccessible waters. The repertoire is also like that. Bringing these works out into the open is probably the most important thing I can do. I have young children, and that has made me conscious of the fact that I want to look back on my career and feel like I did something worthwhile. Rerecording the warhorses of the repertoire yet again seems wasteful and trite.

How confident were you when you decided to bring Antoine Reicha's piano music to public attention. Wasn't this a career risk?

It didn't feel particularly risky. It felt like a logical continuation of everything I had done. I was mostly confident because the music is superb and this is something record companies should have identified decades ago. I have great freedom to recreate the works, and also a sense of heightened responsibility. But as time goes on it matters less to me whether other people agree, because few people have what it takes to discern quality.

You have done little ensemble work recently. What makes you focus on solo repertoire?

The collaborations early in my career led to disillusionment. I came to believe that most musicians are lazy, unreliable, and intellectually limited. Or maybe I'm a sociopath. Either way, I adore working alone, and it seems to work for me.

Do you aspire to compose or conduct?

There are so many pianists out there who are poor conductors that it has become a cliché. I hope I don't fall into the trap of thinking I can just wave my arms and get away with it, and no one will notice. I do write solo piano music, and it's better than a lot of the piano music that people send me, but it's certainly not as good as the best music I am sent. People tend to romanticize how creative composing is. For me the important thing is the connection with music. Everything else is secondary.

Melinda Bargreen

Hairs flicks and mini-skirts

To what degree is music criticism today a force for good... or evil?

These days, I wonder whether music criticism can be described as a "force" at all - given the relentless slide downward of print media, and the inability of electronic media to give readers real insight into great performances and new talent.

What is the impact on performers?

The decline of print journalism is disastrous. Unless you played your cello at the royal wedding, or just won a prestigious competition, how is a player going to make a career when there isn't a reliable source to say how good you are?

But generally speaking, don't serious critics contribute to goodness?

We all like to think of music criticism as bringing to light wonderful talent, participating in the thrill of discovery, giving readers the chance to be in on something exceptional. Or the "calling out" of an over-hyped phenomenon that's not really worth the kudos. But there are times when it also is a force for evil. Over-praise for the undeserving, under-praise (or no notice at all) for the venturesome.

What is the critic's role in this circumstance?

At the very least, the reviewer/critic ought to be able to tell the reader more or less exactly what went on in the concert, how good or how horrible it was, and precisely why that judgment was formed.

Don't you worry about the artist's feelings?

I think that the minute you start thinking about how the artist will feel when he/she reads the review, you are heading down a dangerous path. A critic's responsibility is to the reader and to the audience, not to the artist, except that the critic owes the artist a fair and honest hearing.

You must have found yourself in a difficult position, when second-tier pianists turned up with too many bad habits, hammering the clavier for two hours. How do you stay true to your kind self?

Usually there are two ways to steer a review: the pianist was having an intermittently off night, or the pianist should go out and shoot himself/herself. I mainly prefer the former.

Melinda Bargreen

How do bad recitals affect you?

I've seldom heard a completely awful piano recital. What's usually the case is that you hear routine ho-hum Schumann and dutiful Mozart, and then maybe some Scriabin that makes you stand up and cheer. And sometimes it is impossible to be kind and still tell the truth. In that case, truth wins.

Have you ever acted on the impulse, common to New York critics, "Aha, I've been waiting for decades for someone this bad!"

You don't have to wait for decades! Bad performers come along all the time. What bothers me the most is when a much-hyped performer turns out to be terrible.

I once wrote about a violinist that he "fairly butchered" a Beethoven sonata. I still feel bad, 40 years later. You received a bag of hostile mail after you slammed Andrea Bocelli. Should a critic care about wreckage he or she leaves behind?

In the case of Bocelli, I doubt that he ever heard about the unimpressed reception he got in Seattle; he could hear the roars of approval from the audience and if his handlers were smart, they didn't show him negative reviews. So I have no concerns about wreckage.

What is your view of stage antics of ambitious pianists - the swoons and hair-flicks (Khatia Buniatishvili), the miniskirts and six-inch heels (Yuja Wang), the eye makeup and winks to the audience (Lang Lang)?

It's all show-biz. All three of those pianists, though, really CAN play (though in varying degrees of success in varying repertoire). No matter how short Yuja Wang's vestigial swath of skirt becomes, no matter how vertiginous her high heels, she knows her way around the ivories (I especially like her Prokofiev), and I think she makes music more fun for a wide variety of listeners. If she couldn't play, all the short skirts in Christendom couldn't save her career. Same goes with the emoting of Buniatishvili, and, of course, most of all, the ultimate showman, Mr. Lang, the classical world's answer to Liberace.

Are the Chinese invading us with intent? Some 40 million of their young are working on 'our' repertoire? Are they mechanical players or true artists?

I think it's their turn to discover classical music, and I just hope they leave a little room for non-Asians in the cut-throat world of music festivals, auditions, competitions, and orchestra seats. After all, we Americans horned in pretty thoroughly on what was originally a European tradition (classical music and the piano recital).

But my view of all musicians, including Chinese newcomers, is based on talent and musicianship: if they can really play, let them!

Should Western musicians be afraid, even very afraid?

I think all musicians should be very afraid that classical music is continually being marginalised in our society, with university music departments shrinking and younger listeners/performers hampered by a lack of music education in the public schools. These are worse problems for the West than an influx of gifted musicians from another part of the world.

How adaptable are you in today's changing music scene? What is your view on some of the contemporary works - such as John Luther Adams, John Cage, or Stockhausen, or Berio? What happens to your gut when you hear my favourite, Salvatore Sciarrino's 'Due Notturni Crudelli Il Furio, metallo'?

I consider myself adaptable and ready to be convinced by something good. By this I mean something that communicates to the listener something beyond the personal distress of the composer. How old-fashioned to still be looking for beauty!

And as for my favourite, Sciarrino?

The Sciarrino piece deserves the "Crudelli" designation, in my opinion. We may be better off not discussing what I feel in my gut, but my ears are definitely saying "No, thank you."

Women conductors are mounting the podium more and more in the past ten years. Are the guys in the band gritting their teeth? Is this a fad?

Well, today the "guys in the band" include a whole lot of "gals in the band"; I think the Seattle Symphony is about one-third women, possibly more, and they're certainly not alone in that demographic trend. Women conductors who know their stuff and prove their worth are generally welcomed by players who are grateful for good artistic leadership. Maybe there are grumblings and mumblings among the players, but by and large - at least in Seattle - the "chicks with sticks" are accorded equal respect when they prove they deserve it. I'm also noticing more and more women hired in important principal spots in major orchestras. Again, this makes sense whenever it's deserved.

What are your thoughts on the future of live classical music? Looking out across your audiences, isn't most of the hair white or blue? What happens when they die?

Despite the fact that I share that white hair (carefully coloured blonde), I feel pretty optimistic about the future of live classical music. It cannot thrive without community involvement, philanthropy, and visionary leadership.

Those are always vulnerable to financial vagaries and limitations. Nobody has a great crystal ball with respect to any of the arts but I'm hopeful that the current programmes of inexpensive tickets for the young will play a part in starting future listeners out on the right path.

And the worries about ageing audiences?

If you look to the past, the people who had the discretionary income and the time to attend classical events have always tended toward the upper end of the age spectrum. I don't particularly think that the concert audiences as a whole have aged appreciably in the years I have been writing about music.

François Dumont

The music never stops

You schedule about 100 performances a year. In a typical week, you must be at the keyboard pretty much non-stop?

It may seem strange but I can't really say I have a routine. All my days are different and I am rarely at home for a whole week. But yes, I can spend eight hours or more in a single day at the piano, especially if I am working on new repertoire.

What are your practicing habits?

I enjoy practicing in the morning and late at night. I find the quality of silence at night very inspiring, especially for slow or meditative work. The silence has an influence over the quality of sound, which after all is merely the vibration of air. For this purpose I have two pianos, one of which is in the basement so I can practice without disturbing anybody.

We have heard you perform on unfamiliar pianos in drafty venues. How do you adapt so effectively?

On concert tours, whether for a recital or with an orchestra, I always like to spend some time alone in the hall with the piano. One has to feel the instrument, understand its qualities and weaknesses, and make the sound one's own.

Your repertoire seems remarkably extensive for such a young pianist. What composer has been most challenging for you?

Great virtuoso works like the Liszt operatic transcriptions - I am thinking of the Tannhaüser overture, the Guillaume Tell overture or Reminiscences of Norma - are of course very challenging physically. The limits of the piano are always pushed further. Nevertheless, they are well written for the instrument.

You seem to favour Mozart and Beethoven. Do you have a special affection or admiration for one composer or one period?

Indeed I have been spending a lot of time with Mozart. His music is vital for me, just like Beethoven and Chopin. But it is impossible for me to choose a favourite among the variety of composers available to us. A pianist has access to more than three centuries of music. This is a very special privilege.

On our powerful modern instruments, so ubiquitous in concert halls, don't all top pianists risk sounding the same regardless of the composer's era?

No. I try to vary my approach of the instrument depending on the period and the style.

Most of the music we perform is not actually written for the modern piano, so you constantly have to adapt with balance, type of sonorities, pedalling...

Where does contemporary composition fit into your interests? Do you have contact with any living composers?

I am very interested in contemporary music. Working with a living composer is a great experience for an interpreter - one can make a direct link between the written score and the composer's wishes. I had the immense privilege of playing for Henri Dutilleux his *Jeu des contraires* a few years before he passed away. This was an incredible moment. I have often performed works of Eric Tanguy, a good friend, and I have enjoyed performing and working with living composers such as Pascal Dusapin, Tristan Murail, Nicolas Bacri, Alain Gaussin, among others.

As you continue to grow as a musician, what repertoire helps you develop your musicianship?

I firmly believe that the music you play forms you as a musician. For example, Chopin teaches you the art of *cantabile*. Bach develops your polyphonic abilities, which is for me a fundamental task in the art of piano playing.

How about chamber music and full-orchestra concertos?

I have recently begun the Mozart piano concertos cycle, conducting from the keyboard. This is extremely inspiring and is teaching me a lot as a musician. The sonorities of the orchestra, the structure of a movement, finding the right tempo, the right balance, conveying the atmosphere that you imagine, expressing the right emotion - all these things are extremely fulfilling and exciting as a musician. And I always get a lot of ideas from playing with ensembles.

How much teaching or counselling are you still receiving? I believe you and William Naboré of the Lake Como Academy still communicate, following your studies there.

I am indeed much in contact with William Naboré at the International Piano Academy on Lake Como. We are both busy and we travel a lot but when we find the time, I love to go to Rome to see him and play new repertoire, and discuss it. He has an incredible ear and culture, and he knows me so well.

What are the pleasures and pains of rehearsing and performing with your wife, the Irish soprano Helen Kearns?

I love performing with Helen. From a sound point of view, the beauty of the voice, its colours, vibrations and shapes are extremely inspiring for me as a pianist. I love the *lieder* and melody repertoire, which is full of gems. We have to be in perfect harmony to perform it together. While rehearsing, some heated moments may occasionally occur, as my approach is perhaps too analytical for a singer.

FRANCOIS
DUMONT

What aspect of Ravel's life and music did you address in your musical play 'Fantaisie théâtrale'? Which Ravel pieces or fragments are included?

This was an incredibly enriching experience. I discovered the world of theatre from inside, how it works with text and the intonation, how actors move on stage, how to put together the lighting, the sound. Claude Duparfait is an excellent French actor and Ravel is his life long passion. He can sing any part of *l'Enfant et les Sortilèges* or *Daphnis*!

There was a great deal of music in this production.

Yes, and it was fun choosing the works. There is a delicate balance between text and music, and the musical moments always have to be coherent with the dramatic context. *La Valse,* some of the *Valses Nobles et Sentimentales, Le Gibet, Alborada del Gracioso, Oiseaux Tristes, Menuet in C sharp, Pavane pour une infante défunte* are the works we chose, as well as the opening Cadenza of the Left Hand Concerto.

Are you seeking to build a reputation beyond Europe? Do you have plans or aspirations to return to the United States in solo or ensemble or with a major orchestra?

Yes, I am very interested in performing and building a reputation outside Europe. I have performed in China, and in South Korea for the Beethoven piano concerto No. 5 and some solo recitals.

Philippe Bianconi

With age, we gain lucidity

Do you have a "relationship" with your personal piano, as Angela Hewitt had with her Fazioli (her 'best friend') until the German movers accidentally dropped it and smashed it?

I like my piano a lot. I have a Steinway B at home. But stil it's just a tool. It's not the same kind of relationship a violinist or cellist might have with their instrument, since they perform with them on stage.

Now that you are a Cliburn Junior juror, what's your feeling about the big trends? Twenty out of twenty-four players in your competition were of Asiatic origin. Is this the future we are witnessing?

How times have changed… I have a significant proportion of Asian students in my class and elsewhere. Just thirty or forty years ago we used to say the Asians (mostly Japanese girls at the time) were very disciplined, very strong technically, but lacking in depth and sensitivity - failing to understand Western classical music. But in recent years we can see proof that those clichés are finished, and nobody disputes this. The Asian understanding of music, the players' sensitivity, musical intelligence, flair and their ardent temperament are the equal of the young Western musicians. These Cliburn juniors are as good in their teens as our generation was at 20 or 25.

How are you affected personally, as a professor and a juror, watching the outside world encroach on our Western canon?

I am sometimes moved to tears while listening to these young Asian musicians. There is no more East-West barrier. Indeed, today we find in all countries, all cultures, young players who display qualities to become great musicians. And while I do not approve of all aspects of globalisation, in the music world we can only rejoice.

Still, it's disorienting, isn't it, to imagine the piano world in the U.S. and Europe becoming dominated by Asians?

Yes, there are few, very, very few young Americans at this level. The panorama of piano music will in ten or twenty years be largely dominated by Asians.

How about audiences in the Western world?

American audiences are extremely variable - as are those in Europe, by the way. Some have a wonderfully developed music culture. Others have trouble getting beyond Chopin. But they are all extremely enthusiastic.

What guidelines do you tend to follow in attracting your audience?

A player owes it to the public to be true to himself and to the composer's intentions. He must give life to the music and convince all listeners - to touch them, to move their emotions and perhaps to allow them to discover that they appreciate certain things they didn't expect to like.

You have written that you decided at the age of seven to dedicate yourself to the piano. How could this be true? Your parents were not musicians.

My parents were not musicians but they were great music-lovers. They had a collection of the best piano performances available on vinyl - Wilhelm Kempff, Rubenstein, Lipatti, among others. I was still a baby when I started hearing this music. I remember loving the Tchaikovsky concertos, the Beethoven Fifth, and also the Rachmaninoff Second.

What were your first steps toward actually learning the piano?

At about age six, I began contact with a piano teacher who lived in the neighbourhood. We had no piano at home, so she drew two octaves on a large sheet of paper, with the names of the notes written in, and I started picking out imaginary melodies. After three weeks of this, my parents acquired a second-hand upright. I can hardly express the happiness I felt when the piano arrived.

Eventually you were accepted as a seven-year-old at the Conservatoire de Nice, where three years later you studied with Mme. Delbert-Février. I believe she was 'incredibly demanding'. How so?

Demanding in every way, but she was a great musician and she gave me a very good foundation. She had studied with Marguerite Long at the conservatoire and with Robert Casadesus.

What finer points did she emphasise in her teaching?

When I started working with her at the age of 10, right away she started talking to me about tone, phrasing and interpretation. Until then I had been told to play loudly when the composer marked "*forte*" and to play softly when the markings called for "*piano*", with some *crescendos* and *diminuendos* in between. Suddenly this was a new universe for me. Sometimes it was difficult for a ten-year-old to grasp exactly what she wanted. I felt at certain points that I would never succeed. I owe her an enormous amount.

PHILIPPE BIANCONI

You seem to have suffered by not attending the Paris Conservatory.

In a certain way, yes. But in Nice, I had the good fortune to study with Madame Delbert-Février. Then upon finishing my studies in Nice, it would have been natural for me to transfer to Paris. But as it happened, I was introduced to Gaby Casadesus, the widow of Robert Casadesus. She was a great pianist but at that time it was difficult for the wife to be noticed for her own talents. So she was living in the shadow of her husband.

What did you miss in your education by skipping Paris?

In these big institutions one meets and competes with other young musicians in whom one can find inspiration, and friendships that can last a lifetime. One can learn an enormous amount through these contacts, and find many opportunities to develop ensemble playing. Much of my education was accomplished alone.

What was the big difference between the Nice and Paris conservatories?

This was a case of what we call in France the regional conservatories. You would graduate at a perfectly acceptable level but to finish your growth you would need the exposure to one of the great institutions. Me, I felt I needed to study outside the conservatory world, with someone with different horizons. But I did not find myself in a new world of music. It was more a deepening of my musical life. I needed to broaden my education, and my professors up to that point didn't have the background to steer me forward. In my new studies the exposure to new ways of understanding music was absolutely passionate for me.

Chronologically, where are we in this story?

All this happened between my successes in Cleveland and the Van Cliburn competition. I knew I needed someone to help me work on my repertoire - someone who came from another place.

You worked with a Russian teacher, Vitaly Margulis. Did that change you completely and take you to another place?

To tell you the truth, no. I was afraid I might have to change everything, ranging from pianism to musicality. It was a discovery of things that I didn't know about yet. I was still young and immature. I was surprised that Professor Margulis said my technique did not need much work. He gave me advice and guidance to help me evolve musically and go deeper into an understanding of the music. It was absolutely thrilling. This happened two years before the Cliburn, and I prepared for the competition with him.

You have said that you are plagued by doubts. Is this true?

Of course I am plagued by doubts. This is part of the artist's life. But I continue to work and perform. I have moments of depression but I try to transform these doubts into positives. Many artists have these doubts. Some don't talk about it. But doubt is always there.

How has your repertoire evolved over your long career ?

It hasn't really evolved since my teens but it has developed considerably. I have taken the "seeds" and helped them deepen and broaden. As an adolescent I loved Chopin - not very original, I know - and my interest in him has never flagged. But I have focused more on the late Chopin (after 1840, approximately). At that stage, his language became marvellously fascinating and incredibly 'modern'.

Do you find that your technique is still as strong as you wish it to be? How much practicing do you need compared to the past?

I try to practice five or six hours a day, as I always have, except when I am travelling. It's essential if one is to maintain a high level of performance. I think my technique is better today than in my younger years. I have spent my life working on it, analysing the difficulties and seeking solutions.

Is age a blessing or a curse in this world of the piano?

I find that it is in some ways more difficult to play now than in my youth. Why? Probably because one loses one's insouciance as one grows older, and this youthful freedom helped overcome obstacles. With age, we gain in lucidity but we add new demands upon ourselves. Paradoxically this makes things more difficult.

Where are the Germans in your musical life?

I loved Schumann at an early age and he has become an indispensable part of my range today. I cannot imagine life without Schumann. Schubert and Brahms have also become very important for me. Beethoven too, but less regularly. I always wonder if I am doing him justice.

What objectives do you hope to accomplish in the time you have remaining?

To be perfectly honest, I have not set myself specific objectives, for if I failed to meet them, I would have regrets. There are still many works I want to master. I want to explore the most diverse periods possible. Shifting from one era to another, from one style to another - that's what I find extraordinarily refreshing. I don't want to concentrate on two or three things and neglect the rest. If that hurts my image, well too bad!

Boris Bergmann

Unlocking music in the unconscious mind

Besides being an accomplished pianist, you are also a punk rock and heavy metal drummer. Does it enrich you, compared to the piano works of Brahms, Chopin, Debussy, Ravel and Stravinsky?

Rock drumming is an ecstatic experience. It is like dancing with the instrument. Every hit evolves from a motion of the whole body. Some piano works come close to this feeling, for example Ravel's Toccata or the "precipitato" finale of Prokofiev's Sonata No. 7.

Your career has bounced from classical training to 'new music' to jazz and back to classical. Have you settled on one mode?

No, I have not settled on one mode. Different styles of music still fascinate me.

The compositional methods of your Sonata No. 3 "Hölderlin" are, I believe, unique, editing your taped improvisations. You captured some of the musical fragments lodged in your unconscious mind. Was that your aim?

Ultimately, this was exactly the aim, to capture creations of the unconscious mind. The second aim was to combine these creations into a consistent musical form. I had accumulated several hours of improvisational material, most of it not particularly interesting. But certain passages revealed a style or a musical language that I could not identify as deliberate or pre-existing in my works. It just happened. My conscious mind was not involved. These moments could be considered expressions of the unconscious mind. From this perspective, I look at the sonata as a successful experiment.

How fresh did your improvisations sound after the two-year interval? Did you have any memory of having played them, or was it more like some other person had made the recordings?

I have no exact memory of playing them. I remember the place and the circumstances. I was reading the Peter Härtling book on the poet Hölderlin. After two years the music sounded really fresh, so I thought it could be worth developing further. But it was not like another person; it was more like being surprised, what I heard on those tapes. There were many hours of intuitive work, many hours of difficult transcription from tape, note by note, and there were hours of listening to material half asleep.

BORIS BERGMANN

How much additional editing was required to complete the sonata? Did you have to write transitions, modulations, rearrange the pieces or develop ideas?

In the editing process I barely expanded the original material but in the first and third movements I transposed some parts. The third repetition of the rondo theme (movement 3) shows a variation of the accompaniment of the left hand. Everything else is transcribed note by note from the improvisations.

Examples?

Working with the original material, I used transposition (semitone and octave), repetition and - in movement No. 3 - variation of left hand accompaniment. Furthermore I doubled some notes (octaves, thirds) as kind of orchestration changes and I used a variation of a short right hand melody in one transition of the 3rd movement. But in this rondo movement there is another transition I had to expand its length. Two bars were composed especially for this transition.

The use of magnetic tape clips is nothing new but I believe you are the first to reconstruct your unconscious improvisations into a coherent sonata structure.

It was not my aim to be the first. My aim was to create an authentic and personal style. Of course it's exciting to be the first person to do this or that, no question.

Are you a nocturnal composer?

Yes and no. When recording the Hölderlin/Scriabin pieces I was filming with a video camera simultaneously. The plan was to make a video of a couple of the Preludes. The room had to be darkened, because the altering daylight was too difficult to handle. So I spent three days in a dark room with a tiny light, just enough for the camera. I realized that I played differently in the twilight somehow. And I frequently spend nights altering natural sounds with the use of plug-ins, combining them with beats that I play or programme by myself. Together with my partner Silvina Buchbauer, who is an actress and a singer, we adapt programmes to old German chansons by Friedrich Hollaender, Edmund Nick, Kreisler and others.

What is your involvement with Indian music? Is it the raga scales and compositional rules that attracted you? The sound of the sitar?

Yoga is an important part of my life. Classical Indian music has fascinated me since my first journey to the subcontinent in 1994. These rhythms and tunes sound strange and yet familiar to me at the same time.

You studied at the famous Darmstadt Academy of Music. Did you learn about the greats such as Stockhausen, Webern and Berg there? What did you absorb from their work?

Yes, I learned about the works of Webern, Stockhausen, Varese, Ligeti, Zimmermann and many others. I was captivated by Schoenberg's 'Farben', Zimmermann's 'Photoptosis', Holliger's 'Winter 3' and Feldman's 'For Bunita Marcus'. The beauty of these masterworks brought indescribable joy to me, the pure possibility of creating something like this was ecstatic.

Did you pick up the compositional skills to work in that atonal mode?

Yes, it was useful for developing skills, but the analysis of these works was disillusioning. The score didn't reveal the music's secret. Today, I believe what I learned from this experience was not a certain style or technique or a knowledge about form. Rather a sense of colour and form.

You have said that at one point you withdrew from 'new music' because of dogmatism. What did you mean by that?

The new music scene as I knew it in those days strictly avoided the use of traditional harmony, rhythm and melody. It was taboo to use major and minor, except as quotation or in an ironical context. On the contrary I really loved to use all these "forbidden" elements and combine them with more abstract sounds and advanced techniques.

So you were rebelling, breaking the mold?

Yes - the day I realized I was censoring myself, there was no other way but to withdraw from new music. Film music was the métier where everything was possible in the range from simple melodies to clusters. This experience and my move to Berlin altered my mind, and I was able to compose new music again. But I preferred to label it "modern classical music".

You are a performer and a composer. Does one activity feed into the other? How?

As a performer I rely on my experience as a composer: the most difficult part in writing a score is to determine the tempi and dynamics. Sometimes it seems that there could be more than one solution, whereas you can't write *forte* and *piano* at the same place of the score. For this reason I believe that a spontaneous freedom in interpretation is essential.

In your Ostinato movement of Sonata No. 1 and elsewhere you make great use of repetition. How does this work musically? How is a listener supposed to think of it without getting bored?

Repetitions can be meditative, they can be groovy, but they can also be insistent or even manic. The Ostinato movement marks a turning point in the composition.

How satisfying is your film music activity? Do you enjoy the discipline of matching music to specific scenes in the film? Prokofiev made it an art form, learning to time his sequences perfectly to fit the scenes.

I think my process is much simpler than it might have been in Prokofiev's time. Very few parts of a film score are composed today without watching the film during composing. But I never know if the music works until I have seen it together with the movie. It´s quite a mystery. The moving pictures become a part of the score. Therefore my compositions for film are more spare than my other work.

Where do you find the most receptive audiences for your own compositions? In what demographic?

For my own compositions I expect to find the most receptive audiences in places where new music or experimental music is performed frequently. The audience in Berlin was between 25-45.

How satisfied are you with your career progression?

Things could develop faster. But I´m not impatient. In five or ten years I would like to hear my work played by other interpreters.

François-Frédéric Guy

Devoted to music and mushrooms

Can you describe your technique for creating such a stormy opening for the Hammerklavier?

I try to achieve several things at once for the opening bars - signalling immediately the dimension of the complete work, its conquering majesty, and the vital energy that begins to build from those enormous, outsized chords. I try to give it weight and pace, as Beethoven wanted a rapid tempo. It is as if Beethoven was saying, "Let's go conquer the universe!"

You are busy - 50 concerts and recitals per year.

Yes, now it's closer to 60, divided among concertos, chamber music and solo recitals. I try to maintain a balance of about one-third for each format.

Your new career seems to be changing direction - now you are an orchestral conductor.

Yes, I am doing some conducting. I started by conducting from the keyboard, the so-called "play and conduct" format. Seven or eight years ago I started doing the Beethoven piano concertos. I have booked about ten play-and-conduct engagements in which I add a performance on the podium, conducting the orchestra.

Alone on the podium? What drove you to undertake this new challenge?

Actually it's an old dream dating back to adolescence. I started conducting from the keyboard, and gravitated to the podium. My conducting has been well-received so I am continuing.

This sounds like a major exploit.

That's not at all why I am doing it. I merely want to take the public on a journey with me. I find this idea very exciting. It's like a great crossing of seas on an ocean liner. I will be taking the public with me.

I was also thinking of it as a physical marathon.

Yes, both musically and intellectually. It's even more true in a play-and-conduct format because I have to control what's going on around the piano. We must remember, though, that in Beethoven's time all concertos were performed like this. There were no conductors. Same goes for Mozart.

Do you like the feeling of disappearing into the orchestra when you play-and-conduct?

Yes indeed. The pianist turns his or her back on the audience and is encircled by the other players. So there is a sort of fraternity - no rivalry - but it's not easy. But there is a kind of unity, and that's what is so interesting.

You have said that keyboard conducting gives you a new understanding of the music.

When you play traditionally with a conductor, one must be familiar with the orchestral parts while concentrating essentially on the piano part - that's our role. But when the pianist and the conductor are the same person, it becomes clear how completely the piano is integrated into Beethoven's concept, and Mozart too, and then later Brahms and Schumann.

Contemporary music is one of your big interests. You have collaborated with the composer Tristan Murail.

Yes, currently on a concerto that Tristan Murail is composing for me. What matters for me is new ideas in composition that still retain traditional structures. I want innovation, ideas that change the piano and the orchestra. Sounds we have never heard before. That's what interests me.

If you give 60 recitals and concerts a year, can you still find time to develop new repertoire?

Yes, I try to master one or two new works every year. I recently accepted to learn and play a concerto by Enescu. I always try to put aside time for new works.

At your age, do you find you learn more slowly?

Yes, I am 50 years old. But I have many things I want to do in music. I am not stopping.

Are you spending your life focused solely on the piano to the exclusion of all other activities? Or is your mind open to outside, unrelated influences?

I am not wrapped up in a bubble. Nothing stops me from following important events, such as the relations between the two Koreas, and I am very involved in astronomy, for example. I also study mushrooms!

Mushrooms?

Yes. The other day I found ten kilos of *cèpes* on my property in the Dordogne. I have always had a passion for mushrooms of all types.

FRANÇOIS-FRÉDÉRIC GUY

What does music mean to you, as a career pianist?

Music fills my life, my existence. Even when I am not at the instrument, even when I am speaking of other subjects… Through music, one can express things that words cannot.

Alessandro Deljevan

Living life as simply as possible

How do you see yourself? Primarily as a soloist, an ensemble player, a pedagogue?

I see myself as a musician, as a person who spends his life devoted to music, completely under the control of music. How music changes my sleep habits and my work days is terribly worrying but I'm still trying to find a healthy relationship with this problem. I'm sure one day I will!

Name some of your most influential teachers?

All of my teachers have been extremely important in my development. Valentina Chiola was the first real teacher I had, from the age of four. She was extremely patient and gave me an ideal method. Piotr Lachert, a brilliant man with the mind of a composer, he probably gave me the first splashes of madness, in a good way. He was the first who helped me see music with different eyes. Then Riccardo Risaliti, a maestro in a very traditional way. I was extremely careful with each word, and very, very respectful. He gave me the immense culture and love for the old tradition of pianism and was also the person who introduced me to chamber music. When I was 11 years old he gave me the score of the Brahms Sonatas op. 120 for clarinet or viola with piano and that was the beginning of a truly intense new world.

Where did Enrico Belli rank in your learning experience?

I had two intense years of lessons with him. I was only 15 and 16 years old and for the first time I faced the big repertoire - Beethoven op. 110, the Liszt B Minor Sonata, and my first shocking introduction to the Classical repertoire: Schubert and Mozart. Maestro Belli tried to calm my enthusiasm and to give me a different approach to exploit the score to its full potential. He wanted to make me more professional, to start having more control over my body and my instinct.

How might your musicianship evolve over the next decades? Do you have ambitions to compose? To conduct?

I bought a former convent 40 kilometres from Pescara, in Villamagna. It's very important for me to breathe clean air, and live as simply as possible. Life in a giant city full of cars and smog is hard to imagine.

Conducting seems a natural way forward for you.

No, I don't have great relationships working with too many people. I have conducted a few times from the keyboard but I believe that having an intense connection with each member of an orchestra cannot be possible, at least not completely.

What are your career ambitions?

I would love to arrive at a certain point were I can actually decide what is best for me in terms of concerts and programming.

What is your view of young piano talent, including your students at the conservatory?

What can I say? This is not an easy question. We are living a world where the result is everything. And passion does not count for much any more. Why is a young student with talent studying more than eight hours a day? To win a competition. Not to become a real musician, not live his life with intensity and using heart and head with honesty. Education is so important now. The new generation of parents mostly think of the amount of money their son or daughter will make in ten years.

How important is the influx of Asian piano talent from China, Korea and Japan? Is the piano world becoming overcrowded and destined to become more so?

I'm enjoying the amazing growth of Chinese culture for music in general. Asian culture is historic in every sense, thousands of years of culture and history. I normally visit China every year and what I see is people who really enjoy learning. It's such a joy for me. I strongly believe in an amazing evolution of music in China.

In what direction is your repertoire growing? Do you have a preference for Italian style? German? Russian? French? And what era - Classical, Romantic, Contemporary?

I can't say what are my favourite composers; I always have periods for music. Many said I have a strong feeling with Chopin. In this particular moment I feel a natural connection with Schubert and Bach.

Do you ever work with living composers?

I'm actually very, very involved with the young generation of composers. I'm extremely interested in what they have in their mind and how they can somehow "evolve" all the music they studied. I like people who really know what they want from their own compositions. I also had the chance to work with the late Piotr Lachert. He wrote one of his sonatas for me. Piotr was a fundamental personality in my musical life. He is somebody I really miss!

What is your feeling when you listen to your recordings? Pleasure? Pain? Indifference?

I have made 51 recordings, not including 'Vexations' by Satie. That was eleven and half hours of music in a digital album for Aevea. One of my craziest projects ever. A recording for me is a short period of my life. It's such a strong experience. The days of the recordings are so intense that at the end I really cannot bear it.

Alessandro Deljevan

It's way too much for me. That's why I also do not enjoy giving my CDs to friends. Now I am launching my own recording label. I will be in charge of every aspect. Not only programmes but also piano technician, sound engineer, why even the album cover.

Why do you wear woollen gloves when you play in public?

For years I have suffered from Raynaud's Syndrome (numbness in the fingers). Under stressful conditions, I feel my hands completely freezing up and for the past four years I have been wearing special gloves help me at the beginning of a performance.

What is your view of the flamboyant performers, mainly from Asia? Don't they detract from the actual music being played?

The real question for me is where are we going if the young generation is looking for fame, money and publicity instead of striving to become a real musician with something strong to say. In a world where everybody is talking about a sexy dress, or even quantity of notes I am different. I still want to feel like an artist from the 19th century. Looking for beauty and telling stories through my music.

Lydia Jardon

Any artist who stops creating simply dies

How did it all start for you?

I spent my childhood in Montluçon, one of the wine producing towns of France, where there was also a conservatory. I began my piano lessons at the age of eight, but without much pressure from my teachers.

Were you a slow starter ?

Well, I was no child prodigy. It was three years later that I began to understand the magnitude of the task ahead in any rigorous study of the piano. That realisation came as a result of teachers who alternated with me - one was Yane Weltz, the favourite harpsichordist of Wanda Landowska, and the other a student of Alfred Cortot, Raymond Thiberge. I got basic training, overcoming the bad habits I had already acquired. Every step of the way was painful. In the period between the ages of 11 and 18 I never left a lesson in any state other than tears.

What influences do you feel today from these teachers?

They left a strong impression on me. I now live my life at the piano and I teach my students the legacy that they left me - the body is our instrument, the piano only furniture. The energy of the tone, the gradual horizontal force of the fingers exerting forward pressure into the music is the physical 'horizontal' application of the player's body. Too much emphasis on the vertical pressure produces a hard sound that does not project into space.

You entered the Paris Conservatory at 13. How did you manage to impress the judges?

It was the powerful conviction to dedicate myself to the piano that enabled me to enter the Conservatoire National Supérieur de Musique de Paris at 13. And then I entered the next level at 18 also as a '*première nommée*'. And yet my artistic development was due to influences outside the Conservatory - with teachers such as François-Joël Thiollier (who recorded the complete Rachmaninoff piano oeuvre) and Milosz Magin (who recorded the complete Chopin piano works).

Your repertoire seems very diversified. How do you proceed? Do you have periods or cultures (Russian, French) that interest you personally?

Those two great pianists prompted me to rethink my repertoire in such a way that would leave an impression on the history of recordings.

It was with Milosz Magin that I worked on my first CD, the complete Goyescas of Granados, chosen for me by a man who died just after I signed my contract for the CD - Georges Mendelssohn-Bartholdy, director of Vox, then Pantheon International. He had already published the complete piano works of Alicia de Larrocha and several CDs of Aldo Ciccolini. I had to wait seven years to record my first CD, however, until I could agree to be co-producer.

Your discography is heavy on the Russians...

Yes, It was M. Thiollier who encouraged me to work on Rachmaninoff's concerto No. 3, and I went on to record the two Rachmaninoff piano sonatas and then Nos. 3, 4, and 5 by Miaskovsky, and Stravinsky's Firebird, before deciding to do all the Miaskovsky sonatas - 1, 5, and 9, and the final one CD, sonatas 6, 7 and 8. My only foray into French music has been Lucien Garban's transcription of Debussy's masterpiece, *La Mer*, that I recorded in 2001. In 2019, I joined with two other pianists - Alexandra Matievskaya and Lorène de Ratuld - to share the complete solo piano works of the contemporary composer Florentine Mulsant.

How do you see your musical mission today?

My real passion in music is to resist popularity rankings and market forces. In my view, these currents impoverish our cultural richness. Any artist who stops creating simply dies. It seems to me essential to keep learning and recording new repertoire.

Your CD label, Ar Ré-Sé, was 20 years old in 2021. Where does the name come from?

It is a word from Breton, the language of Brittany, and it means "those women". I created the label after my first festival of classical music by women composers on the island of Ouessant, the northernmost point of Brittany, in fact the most northern point of France herself.

What drew you to the rare piano sonatas of Nikolai Miaskovsky?

The impetus came from Pascal Ianco, former artistic director of the publisher 'Chants du Monde', a collection of all the works of the great Russian composers. He was convinced I would respond to Miaskovsky's music, and he was right.

Was there a cultural, emotional connection you felt when you dived into Miaskovsky's complex narratives and heavy harmonies?

Analysing any composer requires diving into his or her soul and culture, and feeling empathy with the traumas of the past. That explains my attraction to this composer.

Lydia Jardon

Did Miaskovsky's precarious life under the Soviets attract you - the "hell of duality", as you called it? He was a friend of Prokofiev and he knew Shostakovich, two other great composers who suffered under this same duality.

They had to compose in code. Shostakovich's 13th Symphony was a hymn to the Ukrainian Shoah, and avoided the artistic slavery imposed on composers of the period. He had to make his music say the opposite of what was expected of him. Despite the panoply of distinctions and honours awarded by Lenin and Stalin, Miaskovsky managed to express the essentials of his nature in his music, producing deep emotions.

What is Miaskovsky's legacy in the current cultural scene in Russia?

In Moscow, when I gave a recital at the Scriabin Museum in 2019, one of his nieces told me the royalties are smaller and smaller lately. His sonatas have been recorded by various Russian pianists but not distributed internationally. His niece says these recordings are not of much musical value, but an exception is Sviatoslav Richter's magnificent recording of Sonata No. 3.

One can perhaps grasp Miaskovky's depth by learning to play his music but is he accessible just by listening?

The grasp of his state of mind through his compositions explains the heavy Miaskovian writing. A pianist rendering the immensity of his musical phrases in one sweep brings to the surface his intangible internal distress for the listener.

Isn't his piano music less known than his large-scale orchestral works - like his 27 symphonies?

Miaskovsky is one of the many accursed composers in music history. True, his symphonies are in the forefront compared to his sonatas that are relatively personal and private. And yet his sonatas require an enormous effort to bring out the essence. My complete sonatas project can only be seen as a long-term endeavor. Unfortunately, outside of Russia, concert organisers are frightened by the idea of a Miaskovsky sonata in a recital programme.

You have organised piano festivals in Ouessant for women composers. Do you really feel women still need preferential support in the current age?

All I want is for women to benefit from the same level of support as men.

Are you interested in conducting from the keyboard, as so many pianists do today?

I have never done it and it doesn't interest me. It seems to me to be nothing more than a spectacular artistic rodeo, not favouring the emotions of music.

What new repertoire do you have in mind?

If I don't discover another composer from Eastern Europe or Russia, I will probably return to my Spanish origins. My mother was Catalan and the music of Iberia is not that far removed from Russian music in the extravagant pianism and the virtuosity.

Jean-François Dichamp

Bringing the French touch to Granados

When did you have the idea of matching up Scarlatti and Granados? Was this a long-term interest or was it a flash of lightning?

It was an accident. When I started to learn the Goyescas, I recall that during a walk in town I was humming a phrase from "Fandango de Candil". And a few seconds later, unconsciously, I found myself singing Scarlatti's sonata in D minor, K 141. I have no idea why these two themes came to me, but they did. Maybe it was because of the very Spanish character of the Scarlatti sonata. It had been in my repertoire for several years and now I realised these two pieces could be played together, with Scarlatti pieces sandwiched between the Goyescas. I read all the background I could find, and listened to many recordings in my research.

What were you looking for in the Scarlatti works?

Sonatas that reflect a dancing quality, a refined elegance. I needed pieces that I loved passionately because my idea was to create a marvellous imaginary journey to the Court of Madrid during the Golden Era. And so I discovered Scarlatti's sonata in G minor K. 8, a slow, funereal sarabande. It fit perfectly, programmed after the ballade *El Amor y la Muerte.*

It seems you wanted to create a feeling of opera?

Yes, I realised that incorporating these little Scarlatti marvels into the Granados cycle, I was getting closer to the idea of an opera that developed in Granados' time - a grand theatrical work and after each act an intermezzo from another era, not so far removed from the spirit of the Goya characters that Granados intended. We can even surmise that in the salons of the time, the Scarlatti sonatas were included in programmes.

You have a Parisian background. What do you bring to Granados to ensure Spanish flavour? Delicacy? Momentum? Singing and dancing undertones? Rubato?

First, I am profoundly European. I have tried to apply the French touch to the Granados style. I have found in his work a great deal of influence from the 19th century masters. In *Los Requiebros*, for example, I hear echoes of Schumann's *Carnaval*. In *Coloquio en la Reja* and *El Amor y la Muerte* there are the chromatic passages and something of Wagner's intensity, or sometimes even Franck. I attempt to bring a delicacy of touch but also an illumination of tone. I seek a sunny but also refined pianism - Romantic outbursts but also retention and the nobility of a *pasodoble* (two-step dance). One finds this fascinating duality in Spanish dance in which a partner seems to say, "Take me, but don't touch me".

JEAN-FRANÇOIS DICHAMP

You first trained as a dancer. Was that an important first step for you in the arts?

I studied classical dance from the age of seven to twelve. I loved the dance. I had already played the piano in public but the magic of dancing onstage was something completely different. I had to stop my ballet lessons in order to accept the young Mozart role in a movie - I had to make a choice. I remember crying a lot when I had to give up dance. This worried my parents. I cried a great deal when I was a child, not from sadness but because I had an emotional nature.

How did dance affect your piano style?

Dance training helped me enormously in my piano work, to keep a certain suppleness and flexibility. When I play Goyescas, for example, I think of my ballet scenes, my movements of arms and legs, always seeking that supple quality.

Why is this superb Granados music so rarely performed ?

The Goyescas cycle in its entirety can sometimes intimidate a musician in recital, and the public might find it overly intense and not sufficiently varied. These pieces are rather improvisational in style and there is always the chance of getting lost. It's very difficult to memorise. Themes appear, are transformed, and reappear in different form. Of the pianists who have recorded the suite, very few have run the risk of playing them in concert.

Have you have done other pairings with unrelated composers?

Yes, I like to create connections between composers from different eras, to show the parallels. And I ask the audience to hold their applause until the end. I have always felt that one hears a work differently when comparing it to the music that precedes it. It's a way of inviting the audience to seek and find the aesthetic connections. And they are more frequent than one might think.

What other pairings have you discovered?

I sometimes play a programme that compares Rameau and Chopin, or another that matches Couperin and Schumann. Presently I am at work on another one using the Chopin Polonaises and a 'mysterious' work by Scriabin.

You have been known earlier in your career for your Chopin and Liszt. Are you in an Iberian phase of your repertoire expansion now?

Not really. I am a passionate admirer of the Romantic repertoire for piano, and Goyescas is a great romantic cycle. The themes, the character, the lyricism, the fevered outbursts, the harmonies, the writing - everything is Romantic in this work. Albéniz and de Falla sought the very essence of the Spanish soul, but Granados turned his attention to the past, the splendid heritage of the 19th century.

You spent four years under the direction of Maria Curcio in London. What did you learn from her?

Yes, I lived four years in London for my studies with Maria Curcio and I continued working with her for several years afterwards. What I learned from her was that music, for her, was a source of light, and she projected this light around her. I remember that in our lessons she would demonstrate a passage on the piano and at the end would raise her head and, with a marvellous smile, would say, "How beautiful that is". Her face was illuminated with pleasure and by the beauty of the music. And she had the power to transmit these feelings magnificently.

Wasn't she a tough, no-nonsense teacher, like so many seem to be?

Well, she was quite demanding behind that smile. She insisted on adopting a composer's style - the Chopin tone, or the Mozart tone. Emotional commitment was also at the basis of her teaching. She would devote a lot of time to a student, sometimes several hours in a row. I don't think teachers like Maria exist any more. Today, everything must be accomplished very fast.

You played the young Mozart in a French TV series some years ago. How did that come about?

I was twelve years old when a school friend showed me an ad in a newspaper calling for applications to play the role of Mozart in a television film directed by Marc Bluwal. He wanted applications from children aged eight to twelve years of age who could play the piano. We had to send in a photo and a CV. At the age of twelve, you can imagine the CV! At my audition I played part of the Mozart Concerto No. 23, which I had been working on, and he said to my mother he liked the way I sat at the piano. The next day we were surprised that he called us and asked me to come back and read for the part, a serious scene and a light one. When he finished, he gave me a kiss and said, "I have my Mozart!"

Where did your acting career go from there?

There were no interesting offers for more cinema, and as I grew up I was no longer the little Mozart. Soon after, I entered the Paris Conservatory for serious piano study. Something new had begun.

What is your impression of young pianists in general? Has the level of playing evolved over the past ten years or so? We hear so much dark speculation about the rejection of piano studies among the young.

My impression is that today's young musicians are a reflection of society in general. Everyone wants to go very fast because it's possible to do that now.

I remember as a student that when I wanted a particular recording I would go to a record shop, order it specially and wait several weeks for it to arrive. But this waiting period was also part of the pleasure, and when the record arrived it was a big event! Today there is no waiting. Everything is just a click away. Is the pleasure the same? I don't think so.

What has been the effect on young people's psychology?

I would say that in the young musician there is a sense of disillusionment - that great pleasure is unattainable. Of course each student is different in his or her enthusiasms but one thing is clear - learning to interpret music demands a lot of time and maturity. It seems the new generations are not prepared for this kind of patience.

Reed Tetzloff

Let loose and fling the music

Which of your teachers have had the greatest influence on you?

I have worked with inspiring teachers, notably Pavlina Dokovska, the Piano Department Chair at the Mannes College of Music, the New York conservatory where I studied from 2010 to 2016, earning my bachelor's and master's degrees in piano performance.

Aren't you from the American Midwest?

Yes, I worked with Paul Wirth for eight years in my home town near Minneapolis, starting at the age of ten. He and Mme. Dokovska had a holistic approach and cared for me far beyond the piano. That really informed my thinking about what it means to live life as an artist all of the time, not only in front of the instrument.

Are there other teachers important to your development?

I was blessed with several other professors at Mannes: studying Schenkerian Analysis with Carl Schachter, music history and a Bach-intensive course with Fred Fehleisen, twentieth-century theory with Joel Lester, and fortepiano and historical performance with Audrey Axinn, among others. And there were so many others - Eteri Andjaparidze, Richard Goode, Jerome Rose, Victor Rosenbaum, and Vladimir Valjarević. They all impacted me greatly. Recently, the pianist and writer Beth Levin has been a mentor and an inspiration.

So many pianists suffer from narrow musical training. You seem to have a broader background.

Yes, what I received there was the sense of an endless quest for understanding the great music literature. I always had the feeling of exploring music on the deepest level and yet always sensing that there is a vista of greater understanding just out of my grasp.

For example?

One of many experiences that sticks out was the day I heard Robert Cuckson (chair of the Techniques of Music department at Mannes) discuss Schenkerian graphs of the Adagio from Bruckner's Sixth Symphony. I walked in thinking I was quite familiar with the piece, and walked out feeling I had actually known nothing about it!

Where does contemporary music fit in among your interests? Do you have contact with living composers?

I have some contact with living composers, and have enjoyed working with Lowell Liebermann, for example. I have also frequently performed works by contemporary American composers including Elliott Carter, Conlon Nancarrow, Frederic Rzewski, and Aaron Jay Kernis.

You have discovered the legacy of Charles Tomlinson Griffes. Do you plan to continue exploring his work?

To some extent, yes, but the sad thing is that much of his potential was cut short with his death in 1920 at the age of 35 from influenza, during the terrible pandemic. The Sonata, certainly his most significant piano work, was written very shortly before he died. He took a new and fascinating direction with this piece, and would have written so much more incredible music as he matured. It's especially bittersweet to imagine the piano concerto he might have composed.

Wasn't he productive right up to this sonata?

Of course. Prior to the sonata, he was writing extremely vibrant, often exotic music in a post-Wagnerian style, which I've represented on my CD by including the solo piano version of the 'Pleasure Dome '. The revised orchestral version of this piece may be Griffes' most popular work. He was a remarkably colourful orchestrator and I hope my performance hinted at some of that.

Do you delve into the world of 20th century music in general?

Yes, beyond Griffes I'm very interested in early 20th century music in general. It was such a rich period, with everyone spinning off in countless directions as they reacted to Wagner and the end of the Romantic era. Griffes - an American trained in Berlin - is one of many examples that fascinate me.

In programming your repertoire, do you set out to please the public or to please yourself?

I think it is some of both. I realise that some of my choices are not 'popular repertoire' or typical audience-pleasers but I would not be satisfied with the programme if I did not feel that it communicated a valuable message to the listener.

Does Charles Ives' 'Concord Sonata' have special significance for you?

Indeed. It is one of those pieces that grabbed me and changed who I am as a musician and as a person - it clarified many things that I want to achieve in everything that I play.

REED TETZLOFF

It's a wild piece of music, isn't it?

Yes, it requires a state of utmost freedom - totally unbridled. It can't be played any other way. As soon as one starts trying to execute the score literally, it's game over. Parts of it are basically unplayable as written, anyway, and Ives suggested that the score was a jumping-off point - perhaps as if he didn't want it always taken literally.

What did this piece do to you as an artist?

First, Ives demands spiritual participation, that the performer becomes his own character in his world (and the world of Emerson, Hawthorne, the Alcotts, and Thoreau). In any case, as I worked on the piece, I felt it was drawing expressive reserves out of me that I didn't know I possessed. I had no choice but to let loose and fling the music out into the atmosphere, come what may.

How do you make sense of it for the untrained listener?

The great challenge, both pianistically and mentally, is in drawing out the lyricism from such a thorny score: it is truly a beautiful, melodic, and deeply moving work. Ives' music has an unmistakable truth to it. He didn't care about rules or what anyone thought of him. He was a red-blooded, baseball-loving boy from Connecticut who loved campfire songs and big band music, and who loved to sit down at the piano and muse on the eternal questions of life.

You sometimes play this 'thorny' music from memory - quite a feat.

Yes, I felt that I had to start playing it from memory to have the best chance of capturing these qualities. Of course, it can be intimidating to play from memory a 50-minute piece in Ives' musical language, but I told myself that there's no such thing as getting lost when one is creating the music on the spot.

What are your career aims? Solo recitals? Ensemble playing?

I have been mainly focused on solo playing to this point, and will continue that - I always love the thrill of playing a solo recital or as a concerto soloist with orchestra. However, the cellist Alexis Pia Gerlach and I formed a duo and will be performing together frequently going forward. Working with her has been revelatory - I love chamber music but had had less-than-inspiring experiences playing in chamber groups. When I began playing with Alexis it was apparent that we were enhancing one another's musicianship, crafting an interpretation together like iron sharpening iron.

Irina Lankova

All at once, music became a friend, a shelter

You come from an unusual family of mechanical engineers? Were your parents music-lovers?

My parents were not musicians, but they were what we call intelligentsia, people who read, listen and think. There was a piano at home, so it was the most natural thing that I started to go to a music school at the age of 7.

When did the piano first become important to you?

Almost immediately after I started. I was very shy, introverted, bored and sensitive, so music became all at once a friend, a shelter, a source of intellectual challenge and beauty.

Were you attracted to one of the big-name Russian pianists - Gilels, Richter, Yudina, Kissin, etc. Did you listen to their recordings? Have they influenced you?

Sure, all of the above, but mostly Horowitz, Lipatti, Gould, Rubenstein, Rachmaninoff and later Sokolov. Their recordings forged my musical taste, made the reference point for what is my commitment to music, the quality of work, the depth of the interpretations, and the attitude towards the performance - respect for the score, becoming a musician at the service of music and not the opposite.

When were you first recognized as an exceptional talent?

Around 10-11 years old, I guess I was playing Liszt's paraphrases and I didn't realize I was playing something difficult, so at some point my parents were told that I should consider this professional orientation. At the same time, I was also doing exceptionally well at school, so my parents were not inclined to let me choose music unless I entered the best college. At age of 13, I still didn't know what I wanted to do. This persisted until the day I pushed the door open to the Gnessin Musical College and from that moment there was no second option for me. That's where I wanted to belong.

Was Gnessin College very demanding? Was it hell on earth?

No, not at all, maybe just the opposite. My four years there were absolutely wonderful. I studied with Irina Temchenko who was wonderful to me, who taught me so much. I'm still in touch with her on a regular basis. And I also was taking occasional lessons with other great Moscow professors which broadened my outlook. These included Olga Tchernjak, Lev Naoumov, Vladimir Tropp.

How did the move to Belgium at age 19 affect your playing? Was Russian training removed and suppressed?

In Brussels I studied at the Royal Conservatory with Russian professor Evgeny Mogilevsky (himself a pupil of Heinrich Neuhaus), so I totally continued with the Russian school. I also worked with Vladimir Viardo and Vladimir Ashkenazy. I was exposed to other influences by living in Europe and going to concerts. For example, early music that I loved ever since. But my taste for a specific piano sound was already formed by Russian teachers.

Mogilevsky was teaching at the Royal Conservatory in Brussels. You had studied with him in Moscow. Was he the reason you came to Belgium?

That's right.

How would you describe the "Russian school"? Do you feel it in your bones? Or is this a meaningless question?

I think it is real. The secret of Russian pianism is probably in the singing and depth of sound, in the rich scale of colors and nuances, and a special expressiveness. We really look for a large scale of colors, from pianissimo to fortissimo. Not being afraid of expressiveness. We avoid making it overly sugary.

On stage, you demonstrate an attractive grace, smooth movements of arms and hands, controlled emotions. Is this your natural demeanor or have you been trained for this image?

The movements come from the desire of a particular sound that I want to achieve: the singing sound, full and deep, without harshness, long melodic lines. So, whatever my arms and hands are doing in order to achieve that doesn't matter to me.

Some pianists fill concert halls with their non-musical trickery - seven-inch heels, bare thigh, hair flicks, exaggerated grimaces, bouncing on the bench. How have you resisted these temptations?

I need to be myself when I perform. I dress in the same style on stage and off stage - simple, classy and elegant. This means jeans and jackets off stage, long dresses and large trousers on stage. I feel good in that way and I don't need to eroticize my looks. And second, and the most important, I think classical music is not about the looks. It's above all a spiritual and intellectual experience. The music of Bach, Beethoven, Rachmaninoff aim to elevate the human being. When I perform, I'm very humble in front of these composers and the public. I'm not flirting with public, neither do I try to impress. Instead I'm putting all my heart and soul into the performance, and I want to share the emotion.

IRINA LANKOVA

Evolution of your repertoire today will take you where - toward Baroque, Classic, Romantic, Contemporary?

Through the years, it seems that I have gone backward from Rachmaninoff and Scriabin, to Chopin, then Schubert, then Bach. Today, I'm kind of turning back to Scriabin and Chopin. And I also want to perform Mozart concertos. If I feel the emotion, I will play it.

You are an avid reader. How do you bring poetry, philosophy or prose into your playing?

Totally. I read all the time in Russian, French and English. Right now I'm finishing the new book of my favourite Russian author Ludmila Ulitzkaya. Of course, I have read most of classics to Tolstoy, Dostoevsky, Bulgakov, Pushkin, Akhmatova. I think it's important to read Russian literature to understand Russian music, to understand the suffering and the spirituality of the characters. I also read a lot in French and English. For me, it's important to go from contemporary writers to the classics and back.

You are not the same musician you were 30 years ago. As you reach maturity, how has your musical approach changed? Are you getting better and better?

I hope so. You develop as an individual and a human being as well as a musician, and your understanding of life and music become deeper and you have more to say in music when you are 40 than when you were 20, providing you continued to read, learn, play and grow.

How much practice do you need daily to maintain your technique? Do you spend all day at the keyboard?

No no. If I did, my playing would be very boring. Four hours is ideal for me, but in real life it doesn't work like that. Sometimes it's one hour one day versus eight hours the next. The routine is very flexible. I practice on a Steinway B. It's my friend. We know each other. I can rely on it. It responds to what I want to do.

How reliable is your musical memory? Didn't you faint on stage a few years ago ?

I had a very difficult period in my life that damaged my confidence and yes, I had a blackout on stage. It was very painful. For a few years after that experience, I was not able to play by heart. Even in recitals I played with the score before me. It took me a lot of effort, determination and help from various people to get the confidence back and to trust my memory again. Today, I play by heart again, I feel free and love it. But it's not something I take for granted.

Are you concerned about the influx of Koreans, Japanese and Chinese in the European piano world? Don't they favor technical prowess over soul? Will Europeans eventually be crowded out?

I have no idea. I never thought about that. Some musicians prioritize technique, some others expression. The public will choose what they prefer.

How do you see your career evolving over the next five or ten years ?

I want to continue establishing myself internationally, playing on a variety of beautiful stages everywhere - Japan, Germany, Austria, Scandinavia, North and South America.

Interviews by Frances Wilson

Ivo Pogorelich

Life is always a struggle, so one has to be ready for anything.

What inspired you to take up the piano and pursue a career in music?

It was my parents' choice. One day they took me to the school of music and I had no say in it. I was even made to play violin for a while. Soon, however, it was established that violin and I were not made for each other.

Who was the most important influence on your musical life and career?

Rather than influence there was a fateful moment in my life when I met a musician who taught me and trained me to play the piano, and by doing that determined my future life. Later on I became her husband. Her name was Aliza Kezeradze.

What have been the greatest challenges of your career so far?

Art is my profession, career is my occupation. There are two types of challenges and threats. The external ones should sometimes be ignored, at other times confronted. What comes from oneself however is different. The general principle I followed was not to bite off more than I can swallow. In other words "less is more"!

Which of your performances/recordings are you most proud of?

These are two separate disciplines. Performance is, among other things, an act of a moment. On the recordings, all are my favourite and none is my favourite. All because of a tremendous effort that documenting music requires, none because I never listen to any of my recordings. Recently, I recorded two Beethoven Sonatas. It seems I was able to express what was not expressed in that music before.

Which particular works do you think you perform best?

My loyalty goes to the composer I am occupied with. I do not have favourites.

Do you have a favourite concert venue?

There are various ones. Some are blessed with spectacular acoustics, like Teatro Colon, Buenos Aires, or Teatro alla Scala in Milan.

IVO POGORELICH

Who are your favourite pianists?

Generally musicians of traditional folk music, particularly singers, fascinate me. My favourite pianist is Art Tatum, a taste shared by Rachmaninoff who reportedly never missed an opportunity to attend his performances. I also like Oscar Peterson. I have never heard them in concert but people of African origin have rhythmical pulse unique to them. Music sounds so spontaneous when they play.

What is your most memorable concert experience?

It actually took place after one of the very noisy successes. There was a reception and it turned out that the host, a very prominent and powerful person, had celebrated his birthday by participating in the organization of the event. The entire society of the city was in the concert hall and a good many very well known faces at the reception. There was also a piano in the room and all of a sudden someone pointed to the piano with an inviting gesture, where it became clear that I was expected to accompany the "Happy Birthday" tune. I was mortified as I realized that I had never played it. So I bravely stood up and said "I am sorry but I do not have this piece in my repertoire". The host was elated as no one in the room could imagine that I actually did not know the music. Everyone thought that it was cute and witty and they all applauded again.

What are the most important ideas and concepts to impart to aspiring musicians?

No advice of general character is good unless it is tested in practice. With all the best intentions of all of us and each of us, life is a lottery. However general principles are the same as I believe are implied in any professional activity. Self-respect, modesty, determination, being led in life by a clear heart and mind. One must never forget that life is a struggle and one has to be ready.

Where would you like to be in ten years' time?

Happy to be where I am, God willing. Otherwise I would love to be in Somerset on a sunny day. Although I have lived in the UK for almost 20 years, I have never been there. The name to me as a foreigner evokes fairy tales, as it is acoustically reminiscent of summer and sunset. The name sounds so musical to me.

What is your idea of perfect happiness?

The idea of perfect happiness is not seeking it on purpose.

What is your most treasured possession?

I believe it is my imagination.

What is your present state of mind?

Right now I am sitting and observing half packed bags, being packed for a month-long stay with concerts in China and Japan. As I can see the clothes, prepared for three distinct types of weather, very cold, moderate and hot and humid, I am trying to comprehend it.

Such is the life of an artist…

Stephen Hough

Sensitive but tough as an old boot

What inspired you to take up the piano?

I think the piano was its own inspiration. We had no classical music in my home at all but an aunt had a piano and it was love at first vamp. I picked out tunes on its yellow keys and wanted to take lessons. It was a short step (over a long time) for that to become my career.

Who were the most important influences on your musical life and career?

Definitely my main piano teacher Gordon Green. Also Derrick Wyndham (both taught at the Royal Northern College of Music) then later Robert Mann, former first violinist of the Juilliard Quartet with whom I recorded all the Beethoven sonatas in the 1980s. I was 23 and had everything to learn; he was a great partner and, indirectly, a teacher. I would also cite Alfred Cortot and many other pianists from the first decades of the 20th century whose playing I got to know well through recordings. They were always and will remain my favourites.

What have been the greatest challenges of your career so far?

Just doing it - day after day. Specifically, the extreme contrast between being as tough as a old boot offstage (travel, hotels, paperwork etc.) and as sensitive as a bejewelled ballet shoe when at the piano. It requires a unique kind of schizophrenia!

Which recordings are you most proud of?

Ah, tough to say! The Hummel Concertos record was the first one where I felt good in the studio, despite very little time to prepare. We had less than six hours for each concerto, to rehearse from scratch (correcting parts along the way) and record. It was seat-of-the-pants but I still remember the exhilaration and excitement of playing those pieces and making the first complete recording of works which were absolutely central to the repertoire of Liszt, Chopin, Schumann etc. Later Mompou was a joy to record and more recently my own Second Piano Sonata. It's strange to record your own music…

Which particular works do you think you play best?

I feel as involved and connected playing Mozart and Beethoven as I do playing Chopin and Liszt as I do playing Schoenberg and Webern.

Who are your favourite musicians?

Mainly those who died before I was born – Cortot, Rachmaninoff, Friedman, Kreisler etc.

STEPHEN
HOUGH

I've worked a lot with Steven Isserlis and he is one of my favourites, for personal as well as musical reasons.

What is your most memorable concert experience?

Probably my debut at the Hollywood Bowl when I raced over from Cheshire to replace Pogorelich at the last minute. It was my first taste of the fast-lane, crazy side of having a career. Paganini Rhapsody with Sir Charles Groves.

What do you consider to be the most important ideas and concepts to impart to aspiring musicians?

Study the score intensely then play as if you're improvising.

Where would you like to be in ten years' time?

Same place but deeper.

What is your idea of perfect happiness?

Surprised by happiness when not looking for it - and sharing it with someone else.

What is your most treasured possession?

My sanity.

Benjamin Grosvenor

Deep connection is the starting point

Who inspired you to take up the piano and pursue a career in music?

There was always a lot of music in our house. My mother studied piano and has taught piano all of her adult life. Her father has also played the piano since childhood, and has a keen interest in music, so any musical inclination comes from my mother's side. My brothers all played something, though none of them persevered past their early teens - unfortunately I missed out on the opportunity to play in any kind of family band...

When did you begin to take the piano seriously?

I was introduced to the piano aged 5 but at first didn't really take to it, even though it seems there were things I could do without needing much instruction. About a year later, I found that some school friends had begun regular piano lessons. I didn't like the idea of their being better than me, so from that point I started to take it more seriously. As I moved onto more challenging works, and to those by the great composers, I really felt a strong connection to music, and it was only a few years later that I realised that I wanted to be a musician.

Who or what have been the most important influences on your musical life and career?

My mother was my first teacher. She realised quite early that I needed additional guidance and, aged 9, I also began to have lessons with Hilary Coates, and then soon after with Hilary's husband, Christopher Elton, professor of piano at the Royal Academy of Music. Hilary helped to focus and fine-tune my technical development in those early stages, and Christopher guided me musically through my teens and into adulthood.

Were you interested in other great performances - live or recorded?

Yes, my first inspirations among other artists were some of those whose recordings were in our collection - pianists like Horowitz, Argerich and Rubinstein. I recall at that time being especially inspired by listening to Rubinstein playing Chopin - in particular his carrying of a cantabile melody mesmerised me. In my early teens, I became interested in the playing of other pianists born or active in the first half of the century - Cortot, Rosenthal, Friedman, Edwin Fischer, Feinberg, Schnabel amongst others - and found in their playing special aesthetics, ideas and inspiration to inform and enrich my own approach. I also became interested in other historical performers.

Wilhelm Furtwängler's conducting was a particular inspiration - the wholly 'organic' way in which he applied often acute agogics, always maintaining fluidity, was remarkable, as was the depth of the sonority he drew from the string sections.

What have been the greatest challenges of your career so far?

After the success in the BBC Young Musician Competition when I was 11, there was some pressure to become a full-time performer, but I'm glad that my parents and I resisted this, retaining two periods of a month each year in which I'd give concerts, but with the majority of my time reserved for music lessons and my general education.

How did you suddenly acquire a wider repertoire?

The need to have a good deal more repertoire on the go at any given time meant I needed to make changes to my preparation regime. It was tough at the outset of having to make these adjustments, but I managed to soldier through this period and realised that this was very much part of being a concert pianist.

Which works do you feel you play best?

I can't answer this directly because I don't think about works in quite this way. Rather, I look at repertoire to which I feel a genuine connection (above all on an emotional level). This could be a work by Couperin from the early Baroque or the Berg Sonata. The question of whether a particular performance is any good or not is a separate issue, but I don't personally feel that I'm best in, say, a given composer or period.

How do you make your repertoire choices from season to season?

I enjoy variety from one season to the next - while also striving to expand my musical horizons over time - and similarly within programmes. I can listen with pleasure to a recital of three Schubert sonatas, say, but I know that this kind of programming is not for me as a performer. I enjoyed greatly playing Bach's Fourth Partita some years ago and wanted to play another of the suites, choosing the Fifth French Suite, one of my favourites. Brett Dean sent me his pieces *Hommage à Brahms*, written for Emmanuel Ax as interludes between each of the four Brahms Op.119 works. I thought it was very effective as a set, with the Dean pieces providing illuminating contrasts to the Brahms, and that it was fascinating to have this juxtaposition of old and new.

What attracted you to Berg?

I have felt close to Berg's music since performing some of his songs during my Royal Academy days. I also relished getting to know his Violin Concerto.

BENJAMIN GROSVENOR

I love this rich and dense harmonic world, with its tonal ambiguity, whole-tone scales and chromaticism. It is fascinating to consider that Debussy's *Prélude à l'apres midi d'un faune* was written just a year after the Brahms Op.119. It is an ideal preface to the Berg sonata - Pierre Boulez called Debussy's *Prélude à l'après-midi d'un faune* the beginning of modern music.

What did Boulez mean by that?

Debussy used whole-tone scales and also unstable tonality, evoking atmospheres in sound that had not been known in Western music until that time. Of course, Debussy's work is for orchestra... However, Debussy's champion and friend George Copeland had made a transcription for piano, as had Leonard Borwick. There is a telling quote from Copeland about his arrangement: *"I spoke to [Debussy] of my desire to transcribe some of his orchestral things for the piano - music which I felt to be essentially pianistic. He was at first sceptical, but finally agreed, and was in complete accord with the result. He was particularly delighted with my piano version of L'après-midi d'un faune, agreeing with me that in the orchestral rendering, which called for different instruments, the continuity of the procession of episodes was disturbed."*

Do you find Borwick beats Copeland, or vice versa?

In the end, I feel that Borwick was more effective in many sections (Copeland could be somewhat sketchy), so what I'm playing is mostly Borwick, with some bars from Copeland and some of my own.

What is your most memorable concert experience?

If I had to choose, I might pick out the Proms. I have been lucky enough to have played both on the first and last nights, which are both unique events. Certainly for my first Proms experience as a performer, playing Liszt 2 on the first night was very memorable indeed.

How did chamber music come into your life?

I am increasingly drawn to chamber music. Playing with a handful of colleagues and finding during the performance that we seemed all to be firing off one another's imagination and involvement is a wonderful feeling.

What are the most important ideas and concepts to impart to aspiring musicians?

Each person needs to find his or her way of connecting deeply to music. It could be that a promising young musician listens to the most magical performance of a Chopin Nocturne but is shaken to the core by the last movement of Mahler 6. I don't want to sound in the least didactic but I have the feeling that seeking that deep connection - via whichever route works best - is the necessary starting point. After that, ideas and concepts will begin much more easily to fall into place.

Joanna MacGregor

Cultivate your individuality and creativity

What inspired you to take up the piano and pursue a career in music?

I played all kinds of instruments when I was young, but the piano is like a universe. You can use it to compose and to perform - it represents so many different styles of music from early French keyboard music and Bach, to Beethoven and John Cage, jazz and blues. I've always loved the piano, and loved listening to other pianists.

What stimulates you in your musical career?

I'm devoted to practicing and studying music, mainly. It's the physical and intellectual stamina it requires that I still find so exciting; I really enjoy taking a pencil and marking the score, and spending hours with a work. It's allowed me to travel all over the world, which I never expected, as a performer. I love teaching, and collaborating with other artists and composers.

What were the most important influences on your musical life and career?

My mother had me when she was young, and I was her first piano student. She was very imaginative in her musical tastes: together we played Bach, Mozart, Dave Brubeck's *Take Five*, Beatles songs, and gospel music. Being taken on by YCAT (Young Classical Artists Trust) in my 20s was a fantastic apprenticeship; I built up a big repertoire, and learnt to communicate with audiences.

And any individuals?

David Sigall was undoubtedly a major influence. He was my manager until he retired. He taught me to see the long game and encouraged me to be a curator and artistic director. He seemed totally unfazed by anything I got up to, whether it was starting a record label, conducting or collaborating with world musicians. I've also been heavily influenced by jazz musicians; the way they collaborate, make things happen, hang out together, and support each others' gigs.

You knew the late Pierre Boulez?

Yes, my most treasured memory is working with Pierre Boulez, twice; first on a European tour with the Philharmonia and later with the Chicago Symphony Orchestra. He was witty, warm, elegant, gossipy and just a gorgeous musician to be with, both on and offstage.

Which recordings are you most proud of?

Impossible to say, as they're all flawed to my ears, of course. But for different reasons, Messiaen's *Vingt Regards*; *Deep River* with the saxophonist Andy Sheppard, which explored music of the Deep South; and my complete Chopin Mazurkas. Very early on in my career I recorded Charles Ives' First Sonata, an absolute epic.

Which works do you think you perform best?

I seem to gravitate towards intense miniatures and big cycles - Gubaidulina's *Musical Toys*, Chopin Mazurkas, Messiaen, Beethoven, Bach's Well-Tempered Clavier. I like architecture; on the other hand I also like playing in the moment. I find so much music is a mixture of structure, and unfolding, like following a fork in the road.

How do you make your repertoire choices from season to season?

It depends on the venues, and what I'd like to add to my repertoire. I still learn new pieces - like Schubert's last sonata in B-flat, coupled with some late Liszt and Ligeti. I'm not at all rigid about the number of recital programmes or concertos I'll carry around in any one season...

Do you have a favourite concert venue?

Many favourites - the Mozarteum in Salzburg, the Bimhuis in Amsterdam; Wigmore Hall, the medieval hall at Dartington. Something to do with intense atmosphere and audiences.

Favourite pieces and favourite music?

I always love Bach and Beethoven; I love practising them. I'm heavily into Chopin's 58 mazurkas, played chronologically; rather like reading someone's personal diary.

Who are your favourite musicians?

There are so many. The pianists I listen most to are Edwin Fischer, Artur Rubinstein and Maria João Pires. I adore spending time with Alfred Brendel. I admire great improvisers and slip into their concerts all the time.

What is your most memorable concert experience?

Probably playing the Shostakovich First Piano Concerto at the Last Night of the Proms - memorable for all kinds of reasons, including the controlled hysteria backstage. Being invited to play the Goldberg Variations at the Albert Hall by John Eliot Gardiner was pretty exciting for me.

JOANNA MAC GREGOR

What are the most important ideas and concepts to impart to aspiring musicians?

Individuality, fearless talent, creativity, and the ability to design opportunities - fundamental to building a long career. The piano students at the Royal Academy of Music (as Head of Piano there I mentor them all) come with a very high degree of technical skill and musicianship. But I encourage them to develop other skills- curating, improvising, working with multimedia, commissioning composers, conducting from the keyboard, having a working knowledge of early keyboards- that will help them flourish at the beginning of their careers.

Boris Giltburg

Finding truth in the core of the music

What inspired you to take up the piano and pursue a career in music?

I come from a musical family. We always had a piano at home. My mother, grandmother and my great-grandmother were piano teachers and so my first inspiration to take up the piano was the sheer presence of the piano at home. I was five at the time and it seemed to me very obvious that the piano was there so that I could play it. That's the irrefutable logic of a five-year-old. I pestered my mother until she gave me lessons. She didn't want to because she thought we had too many pianists in the family, but I was stubborn as a five-year-old can be and eventually after about two weeks she gave in.

At what point did you make your career choice?

The decision to pursue a career in music wasn't quite a decision. There wasn't a single moment where I stopped and said, "I will be a pianist." I gave my first concert at the age of seven and then by the age of nine I was performing regularly. Because there was no break or consideration of pursuing another career, it just very naturally progressed from being something I did as a kid to being something I do with lots of love and passion as an adult.

Who have been the most important influences on your musical life and career?

The most important influences are both musical and non-musical. Musically I could name Emil Gilels, Artur Rubinstein, Grigory Sokolov, but also many others, Daniel Barenboim, especially in Beethoven, Martha Argerich in many things. And of course not only pianists, but also conductors such as Furtwangler, Gergiev and John Elliot Gardner and singers such as Dietrich Fischer-Dieskau.

Outside the music world, what affected your development?

In a way, every experience you have, every book you read, every movie you watch, every place you visit, every encounter you have, every moment you spend with friends or family, they leave a mark on you and direct you indirectly and therefore leave their mark on your playing.

What have been the greatest challenges of your career so far?

The ongoing challenge is to play in a way that does justice to the music. With some composers and with some pieces it is easier and more natural, while with others it requires a lot of very hard work and a lot of thought and time, sometimes months and even years from the point where you start learning a piece to a point where your interpretation is interesting, engaging and truthful to the spirit of the music. There's often a gap between the way you perceive your performance while you're playing and hearing it from the outside with more objectivity. This is something that happens almost every day.

Which recordings are you most proud of?

I would say the War Sonatas, Nos. 6, 7 and 8 by Sergei Prokofiev, which I released on Orchid Classics in 2012. More recently, a CD I released with Naxos and with the Royal Liverpool Philharmonic Orchestra and Vasily Petrenko of the two piano concerti by Shostakovich, with an arrangement which I made of his own 8th String Quartet.

Which works do you think you play best?

I have a very close affinity for the Russian repertoire - Rachmaninoff, Prokofiev, Shostakovich, but also Stravinsky, Tchaikovsky, Mussorgsky. So most of the Russian composers I am deeply in love with and I am also very strongly connected to their world, Russia being my home country. Russian literature, Russian poetry are also very close to me. I also have a strong connection to German composers, in particular Brahms, Beethoven, Schumann, and, being quite omnivorous, I also wouldn't want to be without Ravel, Gershwin, Bartok or Liszt. But Russian and German composers in a way form the core of my repertoire and almost every recital programme will contain works from at least one of these groups.

Do you have a favourite concert venue ?

I can think of several exceptional halls - the Mozarteum in Salzburg, the Musikverein in Vienna, the Concertgebouw in Amsterdam, probably three of the absolute top venues. The reason for all three is the glorious way the sound soars when you're in the halls, it's effortless and it's an absolute marvel to experience.

Who are your favourite musicians?

My three favourite musicians are Emil Gilels, Artur Rubinstein and Grigory Sokolov, in all three cases because of the deep humanity of their playing. Their touch, their sound - unique to each one of them but all together extremely musical, with every note capable of shading or nuance in a really awe-inspiring way. To that group I would add violinist David Oistrakh for the very same reasons, and conductors Furtwangler and Valery Gergiev for sheer excitement and colour of his interpretations. Also Sir John Eliot Gardiner, whose recordings of Bach in particular I grew up with and listen to almost every day.

BORIS GILTBURG

As a musician, what is your definition of success?

To be able to play in such a way that makes the audience forget their troubles for a few hours and be transported to wherever the music can take them. On the other hand, to play in a way that does justice to the music, that catches a little glimpse of this truth behind the notes. Of course, long-term the definition of success for a musician is on two levels. One that is measured in concerts, recordings, performances, prizes or awards. But on another hand, it is maybe the legacy that you leave behind, whether 50 or 100 years later your recordings still sound truthful and have value for those who listen to them at that time.

What do you consider to be the most important ideas and concepts to impart to aspiring musicians?

Apart from technical advice which is something every musician works on on a daily basis, I'd say the most important thing is truthfulness to the core of the music.

What is your idea of perfect happiness?

I have two ideas of perfect happiness. One, as a musician, is that moment at a concert where you feel that everything is just flowing through you. It doesn't happen every time, it's rare in a way, but when it happens, the feeling when everything comes together and you feel that you're almost possessed by the flow of music, being a conduit to it, while being able at the same time to shape this flow a little bit and direct it, these moments as a musician are utter happiness.

Vikingur Ólafsson

It takes 15 years to become famous overnight

Who inspired you to take up the piano and pursue a career in music?

I came to the piano quite early - when still in my mother's womb! She's a piano teacher and when five months pregnant with me, she played her diploma recital at Berlin University, so I was quite close to the keys from the beginning.

When did you actually discover the piano?

I started playing the piano before being able to speak (I was admittedly rather slow when it came to forming words), and there are pictures of me playing the piano as soon as I was tall enough to reach for the keys, high above my head.

Who were the most important influences on your musical life and career?

That would be my parents. My mother, the piano teacher, and my father who is a composer and architect. Mum introduced a lot of the Classical and Romantic repertoire to me while dad brought 20th century music to my attention, relatively early on.

What have been the greatest challenges of your career so far?

Finding my way after my years of study in New York, moving to Europe with practically no professional connections and nothing going for me. I wanted to build my career without doing piano competitions and realized that I needed to become my own teacher and find my own voice once I had finished school. So I had a lot of time for self-study and focused especially on the works of J. S. Bach, started my own record company and later also started a music festival in Reykjavík, and gradually began to get more and more invitations to play concerts. But it wasn't always easy.

In what way was it so hard to succeed?

Getting a manager seemed very difficult early on. I sent some CDs and letters to various people but never got answers. I felt the business was simply impossible, that no one was listening, regardless how you played or what you did.

Was there a turning point?

No, but bit by bit things started to happen and it helped me quite a lot when Alfred Brendel reassured me in 2012 by telling me, "It takes 15 years to become famous overnight."

I think that holds true for the great majority of international performers, but not many people talk about it.

Which performances/recordings are you most proud of?

Often I find that performances from the past are considerably better than I had imagined. I'm rather happy about my Bach-Chopin album from 2011 with Partitas N° 2 and 5 and the 24 preludes. I can listen to that disc and enjoy it. For concert performances, I'll mention my first Rach 3 performance in 2007 with the Iceland Symphony and Rumon Gamba. I was actually very unhappy with myself after the concert but today I don't really understand why.

Which works do you think you perform best?

Not for me to say, but I do feel very comfortable in the works of Bach and Beethoven.

How do you make your repertoire choices from season to season?

I try to have a healthy balance of adding new concertos and recital works to my repertoire and to revisit works I've played before. I also try to commission and premiere a new piano concerto every two or three years. Right now, I'm still adding three or four piano concertos every season and probably one or two recital programmes.

Do you have a favourite concert venue?

Yes, my favourite venue is Harpa in Reykjavík. I was honoured to perform the very first concert in the big hall in 2011, the Grieg Piano Concerto with Iceland Symphony Orchestra and Vladimir Ashkenazy, and I still get this extra buzz of excitement when going on stage there. Besides, the acoustics are marvellous, the pianos great and backstage you have the view of the ocean and Mount Esja.

What do you consider to be the most important ideas and concepts to impart to aspiring musicians?

I think the most important thing is to find a way to become your own teacher. For that you have to try to develop the skill to listen to yourself while you play as if you were sitting 15 metres away in the hall. Quite paradoxical. Nothing is better in this regard than recording yourself, whether at home or for an album release. But it can be painful and one always wants to practice just a little bit more before pressing the "rec" button and having to look in that musical mirror.

What is your most treasured possession?

My Steinway B model grand piano from 2009 and my gorgeous Longman and Broderip Square Piano from 1785.

Tamara Stefanovich

Music came to me early in life

What inspired you to take up the piano and pursue a career in music?

My parents couldn't afford a babysitter, so I was attending concerts at the Belgrade Philharmonic from the ripe age of three months with a milk bottle - thus food became an important part of my musical life later on.

Was there music in the air at home?

Oh yes. My older brother and sister already played violin and cello respectively, but it was in one of the concerts that I heard the Prokofiev Third Piano Concerto (a certain modernity was always a necessity for me) and I decided I was going to be a pianist, to the utter dismay of our neighbours who then had to endure the practicing of three instruments.

Who or what were the most important influences on your musical life and career?

Bach, Beethoven, Brahms, Boulez, Thomas Mann, Rembrandt, all sharing a strength of disciplined thought and lack of self-indulgence.

What have been the greatest challenges of your career so far?

My country (former Yugoslavia) was in multiple wars in the 1990s. Having moved from the Curtis Institute of Music in Philadelphia to Cologne, I lost all concert bookings, the opportunity to travel freely and, most importantly, all financial help in the form of scholarships. Everything was annulled as sanctions were imposed on Serbia. My life subsisted on a couple of hundred Deutschmarks a month, working strange jobs, having not more then handful of concerts in almost a decade, eating once a day for prolonged periods of studying and traveling with considerable difficulties due to visa issues. I have never practiced as much as in those years.

Was your musical life progressing despite everything?

Yes but the question of changing the profession was a daily one. I worked but my work was not used - and for me not being useful is close to a sin. Some years later I was offered a series of concerts with Pierre Boulez's Second Piano Sonata, which I had to learn, and it became my inspiration, the re-start of a career and a source of energy for now more then 15 years - the mix of courageous, revolting, poetic and young energy in this piece transformed me and gave me the hope that my talent could be useful.

Which performances are you most proud of?

Playing all Boulez piano works in a series of recitals in the United States, and traveling with my husband and six month-old baby was a tour de force like none other. Performing all six Bach Partitas in one evening in Germany, or Messiaen's Turangalîla-Symphonie ten times on ten consecutive days are high on my list of excitements. Seeing Alfred Brendel give me a standing ovation in London still gives me shivers. Accompanying Matthias Goerne was an experience of an unmatchable intensity and beauty.

What music defines you best?

My CD of Bach/Bartók is where I have produced the truest portrait so far of what is close to me as an artist.

Which works do you think you perform best?

The unpretentious ones that have a considerable complexity on all levels - emotional, structural, aural - and that represent a huge challenge as well as surprise. Bach, Boulez, Stockhausen, Ives, Szymanowski for the moment.

How do you make your repertoire choices from season to season?

In constant dialogue with organisers. It shouldn't be just about me, but teamwork between my curiosity, possibilities of the instrument, the hall, timing of the season and openness of the public. Thankfully I have a wise agent who after 17 different programmes does ask if it is not just maybe a little bit too much of repertoire for one season.

Do you have a favourite concert venue?

Kolarac in Belgrade, loved by Richter as well.

Who are your favourite musicians?

The uncompromising ones - John Eliott Gardiner, Harnoncourt, Boulez, Richter, Oistrakh, Annie Fischer, Rosalyn Tureck, Matthias Goerne, Salonen.

What is your most memorable concert experience?

Hopefully the next one… but recently having Maestro Pollini come to my recital in La Scala.

TAMARA STEFANOVICH

What do you consider to be the most important ideas and concepts to impart to aspiring musicians?

Think about what the role of a musician is today and how you can be at best useful for today's society - for me certainly not playing only older repertoire, but thinking how to link music of all times to extraordinary creations of today.

Challenge yourself by not copying someone else's path, and be more open to creation of today than recreating old career structures. In short, less image, more substance.

What is your present state of mind?

Gratefulness.

Pavel Kolesnikov

Allow yourself space and time to grow

What inspired you to pursue a career in music?

I must say, I don't know... My parents are not musicians but they are very musical. There was always much music in the house, mostly classical and what in Russia is called 'bard song'. There also was an upright piano and I well remember I was fascinated, enchanted by the sound of a major third. But in the end it is a bit embarrassing. I was about 6 years old and I went to a symphonic concert to hear a violinist. She was wearing a purple velvet dress, in an unbelievable hue of purple. I thought I'd never seen a colour more sumptuous... and I decided I wanted to play violin. That's how my path in music started.

Who have been the most important influences on your musical life?

The list of musicians who left their imprint on my playing is long and eclectic. My first great musical idol was Sviatoslav Richter. Of course I heard his recordings very early on, but I really discovered him in my teens. I then first understood what the word 'musician' means. A few years later I was struck by Theodor Currentzis who came to Novosibirsk, my home town, in 2004 to start Musica Aeterna. I never knew before how hard one can work and how far one can go in carving ideas and reaching one's vision. Yet later on I subsequently worshipped Mikhail Pletnev, Dietrich Fischer-Dieskau, then Maria João Pires with whom I studied, and Graham Johnson. During my years at the Moscow Conservatory I was very much under the spell of one of my mentors, Pavel Nersessian, a formidable personality and a very unique musician. Lately, however, I feel more and more that I am influenced, inspired or fuelled by things outside music, be it painting, photography, dance or fashion.

What have been the greatest challenges of your career so far?

To pace oneself and allow the music enough space and time to grow naturally. It is extremely important, but it takes quite some effort to avoid temptations and sometimes work hard against the flow.

Yet a greater challenge is to always try and see - artistically - things as they are, not what you expect them to be. It's hard work overcoming your own knowledge and experience. It is a paradox but, I believe, a necessary task for any artist at some point.

Which of your recordings are you most proud of?

Perhaps, the Louis Couperin disc was altogether the most ambitious and challenging recording project to date. In Russian we say: "To push a camel through an eye of a needle." That's what it was like.

Which particular works do you think you play best?

The ones that I am deeply in love with at the given moment.

How do you make your repertoire choices from season to season?

The repertoire choices are painful... I have a big appetite for repertoire, but a pianist has to set the priorities clearly early enough, as Alfred Brendel once said to me, "You learn to live with the thought that you won't be able to play everything you want in a lifetime." Usually, there emerges a certain theme, or a composer, or a piece which attracts me. I then start searching for a concept that would be strong enough to construct a programme around it. It is curious that at a certain point there is always an element of surprise, a moment of spontaneity when you suddenly see the possibilities that you didn't expect at all at first. It's important not to miss that moment.

What is your most memorable concert experience?

When I was 16 years old I went to a music festival in Casalmaggiore. At one point with few friends we went on a day trip to Venice. As we were walking past La Fenice a friend from Saint Petersburg noticed that Grigory Sokolov was playing that very night. We went in and bought the last tickets. I had not a slightest idea who he was. He walked out on stage and the instant before he started playing I knew I was about to hear something I'd never forget, and that's exactly what happened.

What do you consider to be the most important ideas and concepts to impart to aspiring musicians?

My deep conviction is that no idea or concept of true artistic importance can be imparted or transferred. The real things are those that you grow yourself in your own garden, without anyone overseeing. In that sense art is the land of absolute sole responsibility.

Jan Liseicki

State of mind? Always happy

What inspired you to take up the piano and pursue a career in music?

I actually never dreamed of becoming a classical musician, and I feel very privileged to have had such a natural and unexpected career path. The piano choice was purely practical - it was an instrument that was offered to us by a friend so I could start lessons. Of course, now I can say that I was very lucky because I love my instrument for the endless colours and possibilities it offers, for the many sounds - big and small - and the vast repertoire.

Who has been the most important influence on your musical life and career?

Influence on my musical life and career can be linked directly to the influence on my life, and that has been mainly by my parents, who have instilled morals, discipline, and enjoyment upon my life. I gather inspiration from everything that surrounds me, the experiences I have, and those I encounter both on and off stage.

What have been the greatest challenges of your career so far?

I cannot, with certainty, separate challenges from successes, as these are inextricably linked in my mind. On the one hand, I do not come from a musical family, so I have learned everything from scratch. When I persevere through the most challenging segments of my calendar, they make me stronger, and enable me to know what I am capable of and what I wish to do or not do.

Which performances or recordings are you most proud of?

I have particularly fond memories of some performances, such as the first time I played in Warsaw, where all my grandparents heard me perform in a concert environment for the first time, or my BBC Proms debut in sweltering London summer weather. The way I judge past performances includes elements such as the piano, the hall, and the audience, and these are intertwined with the memories I kept of that particular week - a very large cauldron.

How do you make your repertoire choices from season to season?

As a pianist, I am in the position of having seemingly endless repertoire to choose from. I have certain pieces on the horizon that I would like to perform, and when there's the opportunity to do so, I will add them to my repertoire. Recordings dictate the choices of repertoire somewhat, in that I need to prepare a work beforehand and perform it after.

Large multi-concert tours likewise; these decisions are mutual, made years in advance.

Do you have a favourite concert venue?

I'm terrible at picking favourites (favourite colour, country, person, city, etc.) and this extends to all walks of life. I enjoy the variety of concert halls, and believe it is a skill to adjust appropriately to each environment, from the ultra-accurate 21st century 'high-definition' halls, to some beautiful 19th century acoustically warm ones, to the Italian opera houses which make you feel suffocated (acoustically, of course), not to mention everything in between.

What is your most memorable concert experience?

I once flew to a remote community in Saskatchewan, Canada, for an outreach concert from my performance with the Saskatoon Symphony. In La Ronge, where I performed, most people had never seen or heard a piano before. The concert was packed, the excitement was palpable, and the genuine appreciation was unlike anything I've felt before or since. Falling snow, children in 'Sunday best' sitting on the floor of the school gymnasium in complete silence. A concert I will gather strength from for years to come.

What do you consider to be the most important ideas and concepts to impart to aspiring musicians?

Make sure you stay true to yourself, practice only just enough, and learn about other things beyond music.

What is your idea of perfect happiness?

Enjoying the small things that make life magical.

What is your present state of mind?

Always the same - happy.

Jeremy Denk

A different way of thinking about music

What inspired you to take up the piano and pursue a career in music?

We had classical records at home. I loved to listen to them and dance around to them - it was a crucial growing-up time for me, like a refuge. And there was an old broken-down spinet in the house and I loved to play on it. I had favourite albums growing up - the Saint-Saens organ concerto, one of the Tchaikovsky piano concertos, oh and the Verdi love duet - that was one of my favourites, the one with Pavarotti. My parents were not musicians, though my father played the guitar, but they were music-lovers.

Who or what have been the most important influences on your musical life and career?

György Sebők, the great Hungarian guru of the piano, whom I encountered my last year at Oberlin Conservatory, sort of randomly, when he gave a recital and a masterclass. He had a totally different value system and way of thinking about music. There were so many things about Sebők that were crucial to me, but one of them was this urge to find a kind of balletic parallel to phrases, to find a way to move at the piano that exactly mirrors the essence of the phrase.

It sounds a bit theatrical...

No, there was a naturalness and a simplicity that he was after that I really adored. He had a beautiful way with Mozart that really opened up the music up for me. I knew that I always loved Mozart but I didn't really know why. He used to unpack the simplest phrases to find a tremendous sense of play, a sense of constant exchange, little surprises that had to be dealt with one way or another or reacted to.

Were there other influences you recall?

Yes, there was another teacher from that period who was almost the opposite to Sebők. He was a cello professor at Oberlin and one of things that he talked about was "inhabiting" the music, almost like method acting in theatre. He coached a friend and myself on the slow movement of Beethoven E-flat major cello sonata. We loved to argue, as many young musicians do, and he made us meditate on separate things: he made my friend focus on filling out each note right to the end. And he made me think about the saddest thing I could imagine, which for me was the idea of not playing the piano. He had an incredible emotional investment in every moment of the music.

Were these two approaches a conflict in your mind as a student?

No, although they were quite different - one was incredibly European, the other totally American, but they worked because they were both after the same things.

What have been the greatest challenges of your career so far?

Trying to do too much - balancing writing and playing. I would say the greatest challenge is just to play well night after night and to practice well. And having a life on top of all of that!

Which recordings are you most proud of?

There is a quote I like from Vladimir Nabokov. When asked what was his favourite novel, he replied "The one I'm about to write", which I think is the best answer to this question! When I did the Ligeti Etudes it was a very charged moment in my life, it was music I really believed in, and it was fun to work on that music that hadn't been very often recorded at that time.

Which works do you think you play best?

I do a lot of Bach, a lot of Mozart and Beethoven, some Schumann. With a great deal of pleasure, especially for me, I have been doing a lot of Renaissance keyboard music. And through Sebők I am a big Bartok person. And Ligeti and Ives too.

How do you make your repertoire choices from season to season?

Each project comes from a kind of notion. For example, with the music history programme, I felt we all know the story of Western classical music from classes at school, although in the classical world the focus tends to be between 1650 and 1950 and of course there are many hundreds of years that are shunted off to the side.

Do you see it as one story or many small eras and epochs?

To my mind it is like an epic story or an epic poem. I felt it would be useful, as in a time-lapse photo, to watch it go by and feel the pull of time and see all the new ways each new gain or vision of music is also a loss - an incredible cycle of destruction and creation.

Could you cite any striking contrasts?

Yes, when I did the Goldberg Variations and Ligeti Etudes, that was interesting - Ligeti is all about disorder and chaos and a new mathematical order to the world, whereas Bach is the opposite: at the end of the Variations it is all about order and clarity.

JEREMY DENK

What do you consider to be the most important ideas and concepts to impart to aspiring musicians?

For pianists make sure that the left hand is not subservient to the right, that the harmonies get their due. One of the things that bothers me most about young musicians today is the sense of the metronome working behind everything with no sense of rubato. Without it the music just begins to sound like a diagram. But when you say rubato they always think you mean slowing down, but of course it also means speeding up.

Christine Croshaw

Performance success is 'being in the flow'

Who inspired you to take up piano and pursue a career in music?

I remember being fascinated by the piano in my grandmother's house and this led to my mother teaching me to read music at the age of three. My mother had worked in the office of a local chemist, a Mr. Lester, of whom she spoke with the greatest respect and admiration. I had never met this gentleman before, but on one occasion I was taken to visit him at his home. He played some of his precious 78rpm records. By then I was about six years old. Two recordings stand out in my memory. One was the Grieg piano concerto. It made a tremendous impression on me and I determined that I would one day perform it, which I did. The second was an odd choice to play for a child, but I was overwhelmed. It was Kirsten Flagstad singing Sibelius songs, and it was one of the most powerful musical experiences of my life. The intensity of her magnificent voice and the vivid colours of this unfamiliar music made a huge impression on me. I never saw Mr. Lester again, but he brought magic into my life.

By now, you were attracted to the piano. When did you perform in public for the first time?

I gave my first performance at the age of seven and the feeling of engaging with an audience and sharing this magical world of music was exhilarating. I knew, without a doubt, that I wanted to be a pianist.

Did you have a model pianist in mind?

Yes, further inspiration came from my reading of Prelude, a book based on the early life of Eileen Joyce, who was the most famous concert pianist at that time in Britain. I was captivated by this account of a child from a very ordinary background being swept into the exciting world of music. I devoured the stories of her inspiring lessons with eminent European teachers, and the manic regimes of practising, which all culminated in a dazzling career.

What have been the most important influences on your musical life and career?

The first time I heard a great pianist in recital was in my early teens, when I attended a Sunday afternoon concert given by Artur Rubinstein at the Royal Festival Hall. I was mesmerised by the sheer joy and freedom of his playing. This represented the ideal of piano playing that I would, from then on, aspire to.

When did your serious studies start?

At the age of seventeen I entered the Royal Academy of Music where my teacher was Vivian Langrish, a student of Tobias Matthay alongside Myra Hess. He taught me the importance of sound quality and variety of colour, and greatly expanded my tonal range.

You also studied accompaniment with two violinists?

Yes, I think the greatest inspiration and influence on my playing came from the remarkable Hungarian violin professor Bela Katona, and the great Nathan Milstein. Bela had the most extraordinary ability to reveal the inner life and structure of the music, while at the same time demanding a meticulous attention to detail. Nathan Milstein would demonstrate on the violin what he wanted me to do on the piano. I learned so much just trying to develop my touch to match his attack on the string...

What have been the greatest challenges of your life so far?

I had a serious illness at the age of 28, when suddenly, all my joints, right down to fingers and toes, seized up, and I became completely immobilised. I spent some weeks in hospital, where the doctors were completely baffled. They said I would never walk again, and certainly would never play the piano again. Eventually, however, slowly and painfully, movement returned one joint at a time. The fingers were the last to return, taking several months. I gradually eased into playing again, finding my way back gently into professional work by doing a little accompanying, and then duo playing and chamber music, as my strength returned.

Did you drop out of solo performance?

For many years I did not return to solo playing as I had developed severe anxiety about performing from memory. I was now teaching at the Royal Academy of Music, and was also invited to teach at Trinity College, and to establish an ensemble class there. Thus I found myself enjoying a thriving and fulfilling career, performing and teaching, which continued over the following three decades.

And your second major challenge?

Shortly after my 60th birthday I lost most of my sight, due to haemorrhages behind the retinas of both eyes. I had been looking forward to performing solo again when this new catastrophe struck. Recitals had already been booked, and these, of course, now had to be postponed, while I adjusted to a new, and frightening reality, but I knew that, although I had to give up all ensemble playing, I would be able to perform solo from memory. I rebuilt my strength and my career with the support of my husband Ian, and an amazingly loyal and devoted group of ex-students who had become wonderful friends over the years.

Which works do you think you play best?

I think it is for others to express their opinions on this but during the past few years I have felt a particular affinity with the music of Chopin, Fauré, Debussy and Ravel.

Do you have a favourite concert venue?

The Holywell Music Room, Oxford. It has special personal memories for me, and I love its intimacy and unique history.

What is your most memorable concert experience?

When I performed in the Memorial concert for John Bingham in 2005, at Blackheath Halls in London. John was a wonderful pianist and a very special colleague and friend. We had met at Harold Craxton's studio when we were both 16 years old, and entered the Royal Academy of Music together the following year as scholarship students. We resumed our friendship later when we were both teaching at Trinity College of Music. At the same time as John was suffering his final illness, leading to his tragic and untimely death, I also had been ill. Despite my extreme physical weakness, I felt compelled to volunteer to play at John's memorial concert, such was the bond between us. I knew exactly what I should play - the Fourth Ballade of Chopin, a work that had been special to both of us since our student days.

You had not played solo for decades. How did you cope with the pressure?

Yes, this was to be my first appearance for more than 30 years. As the date for the concert drew near, I became apprehensive, thinking how crazy I had been to volunteer. I knew that, not only would I be performing alongside some eminent musicians but that the hall would be packed. The little sight I had left was also highly distorted at that time, so, on the day before the concert, I practised finding my way to the piano. When the time came for my entrance, the most extraordinary thing happened. I found myself following the figure of a woman, another version of myself. I suddenly felt quite confident, knowing that she would lead me safely to the piano. As I sat down on the stool, I sensed her sitting down by my side, and I felt entirely at ease. As I played the opening bars I felt her gradually drift away. I had a sense that all was well, and the music seemed to play itself. Afterwards I received a wonderful ovation from the audience, and I knew that this was a turning point in my life.

What do you consider the most important ideas and concepts to impart to aspiring musicians?

Be curious, allow yourself to experiment. Be kind to yourself. Embrace uncertainty. Do not strive for perfection, but follow your dreams, and move step by step toward your goals. Enjoy the journey. Remember that we 'play' a musical instrument!

What is your most treasured possession?

I have two. My beloved Steinway piano, and my beautiful Cornish Rex cat, Leo.

What is your present state of mind?

Curious.

Margaret Fingerhut

A keen appetite for the new and fresh

Who or what inspired you to take up the piano and pursue a career in music?

I come from a musical family. All of my siblings learned an instrument when we were growing up, although I was the only one mad enough to have taken it up as a career. I was lucky in that from a very early age my parents took me along to all the concerts at our local music club. It happened to be one of the best in the country, which meant I regularly heard artists such as the Amadeus Quartet, the Beaux Arts Trio, Barenboim, du Pré, Brendel, Lupu, Menuhin, Perlman, Fischer-Dieskau, de los Angeles...

Who or what have been the most important influences on your musical life and career?

All my teachers in turn helped to make me into the musician and person I am today – Cyril Smith, Angus Morrison, Vlado Perlemuter, Leon Fleisher. Even my very first teacher, a retired professor from the Royal Academy of Music, whom I remember as being quite strict and rather grumpy, ensured that I knew all the basics of harmony and counterpoint so that by the time I went to the Royal College of Music I already had almost half of Bach's '48' under my belt. And I even managed to survive a few lessons from the legendary Adele Marcus (legendary for all the wrong reasons!), long enough to learn how to draw a beautiful cantabile out of the instrument. A massive inspiration for me was meeting and playing with Leonard Sorkin, the leader of the original Fine Arts Quartet in the USA.

What have been the greatest challenges of your career so far?

Combining motherhood with a performing career was definitely challenging as they are both so emotionally all-consuming. Undoubtedly though, the greatest difficulty for me was the decade I spent dealing with a seemingly endless succession of career-threatening physical problems. Thankfully that is now all several years behind me, and I am back playing again.

Which performances/recordings are you most proud of?

I remain particularly proud of the very first time I played at the Royal Festival Hall - the Grieg Concerto with the Young Musicians Symphony Orchestra, and recorded by the BBC. I remember walking off the stage thinking: "Yes, I can do this!". I was also very proud of the live radio broadcast I did with Leonard Sorkin for WFMT Chicago. I was at the beginning of my career while he was in the twilight of his. I remember the producer being visibly moved after we played the Brahms G major Sonata, saying it had reminded him of Bush/Serkin.

As far as my recordings go, maybe they are bit like children (or students) in that you're not supposed to admit to any favourites but if pushed, I do harbour a particular fondness my recording of the Russian Mighty Handful - such attractive repertoire and much of it still seldom played.

Who are your favourite musicians?

Where do I start? It's a long, long list! Pianists past include Rubinstein, Cortot, Lipatti, Curzon, Gilels, de Larrocha, Annie Fischer. Pianists present include Lupu, Perahia, Goode, Schiff, Kovacevich, Fleisher, Peter Frankel. And that's just the pianists…

What is your most memorable concert experience?

My most memorable concert experience has to be the super-glam concert of film music I took part in at the Royal Albert Hall. The London Symphony Orchestra was conducted by John (Star Wars) Williams and the evening was compered by Sir Richard Attenborough. I got to perform some wonderful pieces, and Michel Legrand had even made a special arrangement for me of his music from 'The Go-Between'.

What do you consider to be the most important ideas and concepts to impart to aspiring musicians?

There will inevitably be times of struggle and disenchantment that can severely test one's love of music. Whatever happens, we must try to keep our passion for music intact whether we are performing or teaching. On a practical level, in an over-saturated market, it is vital to be creative and flexible in the way one's career is managed. If we are still going to persuade people to come and hear live music, we have to find ways to make that experience more meaningful and relevant, be it collaborating with other genres such as dance, the visual arts or theatre, or working with living composers, or simply being able to talk to your audiences in an engaging manner.

About the interviewers

Michael Johnson

Michael Johnson is a Franco-American portrait artist and writer specialising in classical music and culture. The author of five books, his work has appeared in the international press including the International Herald-Tribune, Clavier Companion, International Piano, American Spectator and internet sites including OpenLettersMonthly, Factsandarts and Boston Musical Intelligencer. He served as a correspondent in Moscow, Paris and New York, and was a board member of the London International Piano Competition for nine years. His portraits in watercolour, gouache and ink attempt to communicate the intense emotions of conductors, pianists and composers loved by concertgoers the world over. Michael Johnson divides his time between Bordeaux and Boston.

Frances Wilson

Frances Wilson is a pianist and writer on classical music and pianism under the pen name The Cross-Eyed Pianist. Described as "an important voice in the piano world" (Peter Donohoe, international concert pianist), The Cross-Eyed Pianist enjoys a wide global following and is one of the UK's leading blogs on classical music. In addition to her blog, Frances is a regular writer for classical music website Interlude HK. She has also written for Pianist magazine and The Schubertian (journal of the Schubert Institute of the UK), and reviewed for Bachtrack.com. In 2017 she appeared on BBC Radio 3's Music Matters programme to discuss the effect of the internet on music journalism and writing. In addition to her writing, Frances works as a publicist for a small portfolio of classical music clients. She lives in west Dorset with her husband, two Burmese cats, and a 1913 Bechstein grand piano, known affectionately as 'Bechy'.

Printed in Great Britain
by Amazon

39207274R00066